THE CONFEDERATE JURIST

To the memory of
Dr Geoffrey Marston (1938–2002)
Fellow of Sidney Sussex College, Cambridge
A fine scholar of the law and a good friend

THE CONFEDERATE JURIST

The Legal Life of Judah P. Benjamin

William C. Gilmore

EDINBURGH
University Press

Edinburgh University Press is one of the leading university presses in the UK. We publish academic books and journals in our selected subject areas across the humanities and social sciences, combining cutting-edge scholarship with high editorial and production values to produce academic works of lasting importance. For more information visit our website: edinburghuniversitypress.com

Edinburgh University Press Ltd
The Tun – Holyrood Road
12(2f) Jackson's Entry
Edinburgh EH8 8PJ

First published in hardback by Edinburgh University Press 2021

Typeset in 11/14 Palatino by
Servis Filmsetting Ltd, Stockport, Cheshire,
printed and bound by CPI Group (UK) Ltd,
Croydon, CR0 4YY

A CIP record for this book is available from the British Library

ISBN 978 1 4744 8200 4 (hardback)
ISBN 978 1 4744 8201 1 (paperback)
ISBN 978 1 4744 8202 8 (webready PDF)
ISBN 978 1 4744 8203 5 (epub)

Contents

Figures

Figures

Table of Cases

viii

Foreword

America is, famously, a land of immigrants. That much is well known. What is not quite so well known is that it has also been – at least in select instances – a land of emigrants too. In large part, these have been political radicals of various stripes. Big Bill Haywood, the agitator for the International Workers of the World (IWW), was one of the more colourful of these, living out his sunset years in obscurity in the Soviet Union. In some cases, the post-American lives were rather more distinguished. The scientist David Bohm and classical historian Moses Finlay, for example – both targets of vilification during the McCarthy era – went on to fill academic posts in England. Some fled the uninviting racial atmosphere in the United States. Josephine Baker, for example, renounced her American nationality and became a star entertainer in Europe. The novelists Richard Wright and James Baldwin similarly opted for lives of permanent exile.

One of the most distinguished, and earliest, of these American transplants was Judah P. Benjamin. For one thing, none had held such high political office as he – a member of the United States Senate, and then the holder of no fewer than three cabinet posts in the Confederate States of America, most notably that of Secretary of State. Benjamin even had the distinction of being, at least technically, *both* an immigrant to *and* an emigrant from the United States. The immigration part stemmed from his birth on the island of St Croix in the Danish West Indies (with the island being under temporary British occupation at the time of the birth).

As this book sets out so vividly, Benjamin's whole life and career – or rather careers – were something of a catalogue of oddities. He is impervious to pigeon-holing to a remarkable extent. One commentator wryly remarked: "Hebrew in blood, English in tenacity of grasp and purpose, Mr Benjamin was French in taste."[1] And all this while being the very image of the nineteenth-century American resolutely on the upward path to success. A key feature of this odyssey was a powerful work ethic. To a large extent, he was a self-made man. A period of study at Yale College, commenced at the ripe age of fourteen, indicates his determination to rise in the world – though his studies, which came to an untimely end, seem to have contributed little to his later eminence.

It was largely self-study which took Benjamin to the heights of the legal profession in his adopted home of Louisiana – a change of venue involving, all too characteristically, migration within the United States, from his boyhood environs of North and South Carolina. Not the least, or the least probable, of his achievements in that new setting was emergence as the owner of a substantial sugar plantation, complete with well over a hundred slaves. As an ironic indication of how thoroughly he was living the life of a southern aristocrat, he then lost the plantation, as a result of having gallantly co-signed notes of indebtedness of a friend. He was in suitably distinguished company in this regard: Thomas Jefferson had previously sacrificed financial solvency on the altar of gentlemanly friendship.

The transition from legal and planterly prominence to politics was natural enough in that era. But here too, Benjamin proved difficult to classify. He was a staunch

---

[1] T. C. De Leon, *Belles, Beaux and Brains of the 60's* (N.Y: G. W. Dillingham, 1907), at 91–92.

and eloquent defender of the Southern way of life and the rights of slaveholders, but he was no fire-eating secessionist. When his state left the Union, he dutifully went with it – and, not surprisingly, put his manifold talents to use in his would-be new nation. Although he and Jefferson Davis, the president of the Confederacy, had not been personally close during their years together in the Senate, they became inseparable comrades in the trying years of the Civil War. No one in Confederate government circles was closer to Davis than Benjamin.

The defeat of the Confederacy in 1865 inevitably meant a great change for Benjamin. In the event, the change proved greater than for any other official of the Confederate government. At first, there was some disposition to subject the leaders of the Confederacy to trial for treason.[2] With the eventual discontinuance of proceedings against Jefferson Davis, this course of action was dropped; and the federal government's policy became, instead, one of ever-greater generosity in the granting of pardons to Confederate war participants – to the point that, by the end of the Johnson administration, virtually the only persons not covered by pardon grants were the Lincoln assassins. But Benjamin – alone of all the Confederate government figures – declined to take advantage of this expansive spirit of forgiveness. Instead, he embarked on the life of a refugee, in Britain – a country that he had never before visited.

As this book reveals, Benjamin's penchant for hard work and patience, liberally admixed with legal acumen of a high order, stood him in good stead in his new life in the Old World, as it previously had in the United States. At the English bar, he went on to a career of the highest eminence, attaining a strikingly high degree of both respect and affection from his newest circle of fellow

---

[2] See generally Cynthia Nicoletti, *Secession on Trial: The Treason Prosecution of Jefferson Davis* (Cambridge: Cambridge Univesity Press, 2017).

legal professionals. This is an aspect of Benjamin's life which is practically unknown to American audiences – just as Benjamin's eventful earlier careers are practically a closed book to British lawyers.

To the present day, Benjamin carries on an attenuated existence in law offices all over Great Britain, in the form of *Benjamin's Sale of Goods* – although, as noted in Chapter 5, this present text is really a respectful tribute to Benjamin's pioneering work in the field, rather than an actual continuation of his original text. But how few of today's workaday lawyers have any awareness of the extraordinary back story of the eponymous "Benjamin" of their humdrum daily routine. They – and many others too – can profitably read Professor Gilmore's exhilarating account of that remarkable life.

Stephen C. Neff
Professor of War and Peace, University of Edinburgh

Preface and Acknowledgments

I was first made aware of Judah Philip Benjamin in the mid-1970s in the unlikely surroundings of the Confederation Building; a large and somewhat Stalinist looking structure overlooking the city of St John's, Newfoundland. The Province was then involved in a protracted dispute with the Canadian federal government as to which enjoyed ownership and control of the substantial oil and gas resources which had been discovered on the continental shelf adjacent to the island. Newfoundland had established a small team of academic advisers to assist in preparations for related actions in the courts.

I was by far the most junior member of this select group and was included partly because I was at the time based in Ottawa and therefore near to both the national archives and the Departments of the Canadian Government. I had also previously had a measure of involvement in the teaching of Colonial Constitutional Law at the University of the West Indies in Barbados where I had been for a few years a Lecturer in Law; a relevant area of legal scholarship in the fact circumstance of this dispute. I had two other close academic colleagues in this context. The first was D. P. O'Connell (1924–1979) then Chichele Professor of Public International Law at Oxford and a great sage on matters to do with the law of the sea. The second was Dr Geoffrey Marston (1938–2002); a Fellow of Sidney Sussex College and Lecturer in Law in the University of Cambridge. Both had been involved, on opposite sides, in a somewhat

xiv

similar constitutional dispute which had been resolved by the High Court of Australia in 1975.[1]

One of the many obstacles facing Newfoundland in its, eventually unsuccessful, quest for judicial validation of its claim to legislative and executive powers in respect of the natural resources of the seabed and subsoil of the adjacent seas[2] took the form of the 1876 decision of the Court for Crown Cases Reserved in *Regina v Keyn*[3]; perhaps Benjamin's greatest case in his short but distinguished career at the English Bar. I recall with particular clarity the occasion on which Marston shared with me his analysis of the transcript of the arguments which Benjamin had advanced before the court; his admiration for the breadth and depth of his command of the complex issues of law which that case engaged, as well as his impression as to the unusual degree of deference shown to Benjamin by the Bench of fourteen judges which sat. I there resolved to take a closer look at this nineteenth-century legal legend as and when time permitted.

Some forty years were to pass before that opportunity presented, and this biographical sketch is the outcome. Its focus is firmly fixed on Benjamin's public life; as consummate advocate, gifted legal scholar and influential supporter of slavery in America. His unorthodox private and family life, his religious background and similar matters, are treated only where considered necessary to establish an appropriate context for an understanding of his career choices and his professional development, and to gain an appreciation of the nature and extent of the barriers he had

---

[1] See generally, *New South Wales and Others v Commonwealth* (1975)135 CLR 337.

[2] See generally, *Re.Seabed and Subsoil of Continental Shelf Offshore Newfoundland* (1984) 5 DLR. (4th) 385 (Supreme Court of Canada). See also, *Reference Re.Mineral and Other Natural Resources of the Continental Shelf* (1983)145 DLR (3d) 9 (Newfoundland Court of Appeal)

[3] *Regina v Keyn* (1876) 2 Ex.D.63; 13 Cox.CC.403.

to confront or evade in achieving the success that he had. The footnotes direct the reader to source materials where such lightly treated matters can be more fully explored.[4]

In taking this project forward, I based myself primarily in the National Library of Scotland in Edinburgh. Other library collections were consulted and visits made to, *inter alia*, the National Archives in London and the Library of Congress in Washington, DC; two of the most outstanding research facilities in the modern world. I would like to take this opportunity to extend my thanks to the staff of all of these institutions for their kindness and assistance. I also wish to acknowledge with thanks the many scholars and archivists, several of whom I have never met, who when approached, offered me the assistance which I sought. Among those strangers who kindly assisted on multiple occasions were: Professor William C. Davis of Virginia Tech; Ms F. Bellis, Assistant Librarian, Lincoln's Inn; Professor J. E. Duggan and his colleague K. Glorioso of the Law Library at Tulane Law School; and, Edward Richi, Research Specialist, Delaware Historical Society in Wilmington. I am very much in their debt. Closer to home several of my Edinburgh Law School colleagues, including Professors Elspeth Reid and George Gretton, offered encouragement and support.

Being of a non-technological disposition – part of what my daughter describes as my learned helplessness – the

---

[4] This approach is also suggested by the fact that Benjamin left no personal archive. As his friend, fellow barrister, and the co-executor of his estate, J G Witt, QC, was to note: "Another trait. He left no documents. When I first became friends with him, he told me that on his starting in law business in New Orleans, his partner taught him that the secret of human happiness was the destruction of writings. . ..He did not preach without practising. When he died, he did not leave behind him half a dozen pieces of paper." "Life of Judah P Benjamin Q.C", undated typescript of three pages, but thought to have been written in the 1890s, held in the Bayard Papers, Delaware Historical Society, Wilmington, Folder 55, J P Benjamin correspondence, 1856–1898, Item 14.

manuscript was written by hand. It was prepared for the publishers through the kindness and efficiency of my friend and former colleague Miss Lydia Lawson. My thanks are also due to my wife, Patricia, who put up with my many Benjamin related absences, gave up her dining room for over a year so I could construct the text and located Benjamin's obscure last resting place in Paris. I also wish to acknowledge the assistance of Ms Laura Williamson of Edinburgh University Press who took this project from proposal to publication. Finally, I wish to thank the staff of Giclee UK, fine art printers of Edinburgh, for expertly enhancing the quality of various of the images reproduced within this volume.

While I have derived assistance from many the views contained in the pages which follow are mine alone, I am, of course, solely responsible for any deficiencies of style or substance which remain.

Bill Gilmore,
July 2020, Edinburgh

Introduction

On the evening of Saturday 30 June 1883, a "grand banquet"[1] was held at the Inner Temple Hall in central London. The event was hosted by the then Attorney General of England and Wales, Sir Henry James.

As *The Times*, the principal newspaper of record in the UK, was to report: "It is a beautiful hall, which has lately been rebuilt, and it is adorned by portraits of the most eminent and illustrious of those who have given dignity to the [legal] profession in past generations. The hall on this occasion was filled with a splendid company, and presented a magnificent spectacle. About 200 members of the profession, including all its higher and more distinguished ornaments joined in the entertainment."[2] Among those present were the Lord Chancellor (the Earl of Selborne), the Lord Chief Justice of England (Lord Coleridge) – both of whom were to address the assembled company – numerous members of the judiciary, other Law Officers of the Crown,[3] and throngs of barristers, both senior and junior, including several from the Americas.

This gathering, described by the Attorney General as

---

[1] *The Times*, 9 May 1884, p. 10.

[2] "Entertainment to Mr Benjamin, QC, at the Inner Temple Hall", *The Times*, 2 July 1883, p. 6. The hall was destroyed in the course of World War II.

[3] These included the Solicitor General of England, the Lord Advocate of Scotland and the Attorney General of Ireland.

"[r]emarkable and unprecedented",[4] was brought about at the written request of "almost every leading member of the English Bar" who wished to mark the retirement of Mr Judah P. Benjamin collectively.[5] His sudden and somewhat unexpected withdrawal from professional life was prompted by ill health. It had been announced a few months earlier. As *The Times* was to note on 9 February 1883: "Mr Benjamin has for many years been almost the leader of the English Bar in all heavy appeal cases. His career has been very remarkable."[6] The following day, *The Daily Telegraph*, another leading British newspaper, was even more effusive in its praise. It remarked:

> The history of the English Bar will hereafter have no prouder story to tell than that of the marvellous advance of Mr Benjamin from the humble position he occupied as a junior in 1866 to the front rank of his profession in 1883.[7]

Such a glittering outcome to his professional life was by no means preordained. As will be seen in greater detail later in this study, Benjamin had been born into a Jewish family of extremely limited means in an obscure Danish island colony in the Caribbean from which they subsequently

---

[4] *The Remarks of the Attorney General and the Response of Mr Judah P. Benjamin at the Dinner in the Inner Temple Hall, London, June 30, 1883* (undated Private Print). The speeches were also extensively reproduced at *supra*, note 2.

[5] See J. H. Winston, "Judah P. Benjamin: Distinguished at Bars of Two Nations" (1929), *American Bar Association Journal*, Vol. 15, p. 567 (part 1) and p. 643 (part 2) at p. 646.

[6] *The Times*, 9 February 1883, p. 7. Benjamin's progress at the English Bar had not gone unnoticed in the United States. For instance the *New York Times* remarked, on 14 August 1879, that 14 years after fleeing into English exile "this fugitive becomes the recognized head of an institution of all others the most exclusive and difficult in which to attain prominence and success – the Bar of England".

[7] 10 February 1883, p. 5.

emigrated to the United States. There Benjamin eventually fashioned a career first in the legal profession and thereafter in political life. Upon the secession of the Southern States, he sided with the Confederacy which he served in several high profile Cabinet-level roles including those of Attorney General and Secretary of State. In the Spring of 1865 and in anticipation of the imminent surrender of General Lee at Appomattox, he fled first the Confederate capital of Richmond and then the country never to return. Rather, after a difficult and daring escape, he sought sanctuary in the United Kingdom whence he arrived in late August of the same year. In London he started life afresh and nearly from scratch as his wealth, which was by no means insignificant, had been confiscated by the United States; a not unusual, though legally somewhat problematic, coerced tribute of the vanquished to the victor.

In late 1882 Benjamin, who had not enjoyed robust good health for some time, journeyed to Paris to spend the Christmas vacation with his wife and adult daughter who had lived in France for many years. There his condition deteriorated, and he was "advised by the most eminent medical authorities that it is absolutely necessary for him to enjoy complete repose".[8] It was from his Paris home that Benjamin journeyed to London to be the guest of honour at the 30 June 1883 banquet, though his fragile state was evident. As one commentator was later to remark: "he had become very much enfeebled, and looked weak and ill".[9]

In proposing the toast to the health of their guest, Sir Henry James reminded his audience that "[t]he years are few since Mr Benjamin was a stranger to us all, and in those few years he has accomplished more than most can

---

[8] *The Times, supra*, note 6, p. 7.
[9] Anon, "Judah P. Benjamin" (1889: September), *The Green Bag*, Vol. I, No. 9, p. 365, at p. 366.

ever hope in a lifetime to achieve".[10] A retirement event of this nature had never before been held for a barrister, was rare even for senior members of the judiciary, and "Benjamin was very conscious indeed of the honor it signified".[11] If any of those present were in any doubt of "the rarity of such tributes",[12] they were reminded of the fact by the Lord Chief Justice. He recalled that some forty years earlier a similar collective mark of respect had been intended for Justice Story of the Supreme Court of the United States though, in the event, it could not actually be received by him. He continued: "Forty years have elapsed and we pay such an honour to one more distinguished than Story . . .".[13] Even making allowances for the tendency towards hyperbole at retirement occasions such as these, this was high praise indeed.

Benjamin was "deeply touched" by the words of the Attorney General and by the evening as a whole.[14] In his relatively brief remarks, he took the opportunity to acknowledge many of those who had assisted his entry, in his mid-fifties, to life at the Bar and to reflect upon the reception he had received as an outsider within its ranks: "I never, so far as I am aware, received anything but a warm and kindly welcome. I never had occasion to feel that anyone regarded me as an intruder. I never felt a touch of professional jealousy. I never received any unkindness. On the contrary, from all quarters I received a warm and cordial welcome to which, as a stranger, I had

---

[10] *Supra*, note 4. The event was widely reported in the British media. See, e.g., *Daily Telegraph*, 2 July 1883, at p. 3.

[11] S. Naresh, "Judah Philip Benjamin at the English Bar" (1995–1996) *Tulane Law Review*, Vol. 70, p. 2487, at p. 2496.

[12] C. MacMillan, "Judah Benjamin: Marginalized Outsider or Admitted Insider" (2015) *Journal of Law and Society*, Vol. 42, p. 150, at p. 150.

[13] *Supra*, note 2, p. 6.

[14] See, e.g., R. D. Meade, *Judah P. Benjamin: Confederate Statesman* (2001 reprint of 1943 original) (Louisiana State University Press, Baton Rouge), at pp. 378–379.

no title, except that I was a political exile, seeking honourable labour to retrieve shattered fortunes, wrecked in the ruin of a lost cause."[15]

While he took "joy and gratification" at the honour which had been afforded to him, this was more than counterbalanced "by the reflection, unutterably sad, that to the large majority of those present my farewell words to-night are a final earthly farewell – that to the large majority of you I shall never again be cheered by the smiling welcome, by the hearty hand-grasp, with which I have been greeted during many years, and which had become to me almost the very breath of my life".[16]

These words were indeed prescient. Following the banquet, he immediately returned to Paris. Within a year he was dead, thus bringing to an end "[o]ne of the most remarkable of modern careers".[17] In the oft-quoted words of *The Times* obituary: "His life was as various as an Eastern tale and he carved out for himself by his own unaided exertions not one but three several histories of great and well-earned distinction".[18] It is to that wider and most colourful canvas that this study now turns.

Chapter 1 charts Benjamin's emergence as one of the leading American legal practitioners of the mid-nineteenth century. It reflects upon his legal education in Louisiana, his first contribution to legal scholarship and its positive impact on his swift acquisition of an extensive, substantial and lucrative practice initially in his home state and then nationally. It notes his emergence as a plantation owner with a substantial number of slaves and the circumstances surrounding the subsequent loss of these "investments". It

[15] *Supra*, note 4. As the Attorney General had earlier remarked, Benjamin "had to bear the usual lot of vanquished men. Little save honour, reputation, and great gifts remained to him."

[16] *Id.*

[17] *Supra*, note 1.

[18] *Id.*

incorporates coverage of the manner in which he nurtured his political ambitions culminating in his appointment as a member of the United States Senate. It outlines how, in seven years in Washington DC, Benjamin – who had seemingly declined nomination to the US Supreme Court in 1853 – became a constant feature in litigation before it.

Chapter 2 acts as a bridge between Benjamin's two separate legal careers; first in the United States and thereafter in England. Its initial focus is on the political positions he adopted in the Senate on the pivotal and connected issues of the future of slavery and Southern secession. With the crystallisation of the latter it outlines how he sided with the Confederacy, became a close confidant of President Jefferson Davis, and served throughout the conflict in his Cabinet; first as Attorney General, then as Secretary of War, and finally as Secretary of State. It concludes by tracing how, upon the disintegration of the Confederate government in the spring of 1865, Benjamin evaded capture by Union forces and sought sanctuary in the United Kingdom. This is supplemented by Appendix 1 where full details of his daring escape from America are recounted in Benjamin's own words.

The focus of Chapter 3 is on how at the age of 55, in political exile and with limited financial means, Benjamin managed to overcome the practical and formal barriers to his desire to resume in England his career in the law. It examines, in particular, the archival records of Lincoln's Inn to establish the grounds upon which and the process through which he succeeded in securing a greatly expedited call to the Bar. By way of an examination of Colonial Constitutional Law and the then rules of common law and statute relating to nationality it also clarifies the basis on which Benjamin managed to secure recognition of his status as a British subject; then a precondition for Bar membership.

Chapter 4 charts the meteoric rise of Benjamin from a

humble junior in 1866, reliant to an extent for briefs from Confederate contacts and sympathisers, to his undisputed leadership of the English Bar in appellate cases, particularly before the House of Lords and the Judicial Committee of the Privy Council, by the time of his retirement in 1883. The factors contributing to this transformation, including the impact of his 1868 treatise on the law of sale and his ability to turn the apparent disadvantage of his origins within the civil law tradition of Louisiana into a significant asset in Scottish and colonial appeals, are identified and examined. The depth and breadth of his command of the law is illustrated especially through an analysis of *Regina v Keyn* before the Court for Crown Cases Reserved in 1876 – the case which many commentators, and Benjamin himself, regard as his greatest.[19]

Chapter 5 commences with Benjamin's death in Paris in May 1884 and the manner in which this news was received in the media and in professional circles in the United Kingdom, his home state of Louisiana and in America more generally. This forms the context for an assessment of his several careers and of the personal and professional attributes which contributed, often in the face of disadvantage and adversity, to his successes. His legacy, perhaps more as a distinguished jurist than as a somewhat flawed and controversial politician, forever associated with support for slavery and the secession of the Confederacy, is also considered in concluding this biographical sketch of an intriguing and complex figure.

[19] (1876) LR 2 Ex. D 63

Figure I.1 Coat of Arms, Lincoln's Inn. Reproduced courtesy of the Librarian, Lincoln's Inn.

1

Benjamin's Emergence as an American Lawyer and Politician

Judah Benjamin was born on the Danish West Indian island of St Croix in early August 1811 during a period of British military occupation in the Napoleonic Wars.[1] His parents, both from the Sephardic Jewish tradition,[2] had emigrated there from England a few years earlier in search of a better life. The growing Benjamin family did not stay long. In 1813 they moved on to North Carolina where his father "continued his uniformly unsuccessful business career"[3]. By 1822 the family was based in Charleston, South Carolina where Benjamin Sr ran a small "dry goods" store.[4]

Though his family's financial circumstances throughout this period were very challenging, Judah Benjamin attended school continuously and proved to be something of a natural child scholar. In 1825, at the age of fourteen, he was admitted to Yale, the first Jewish student in many years to attend that outstanding university.[5] At New

---

[1] He was the third child. Further siblings were to follow. See, e. g., J. A. Hamilton, revised by H. C. G. Matthew, Benjamin, Judah Philip, *Oxford Dictionary of National Biography (online edition)*.

[2] See, e.g., R. D. Meade, *Judah P. Benjamin: Confederate Statesman* (2001 reprint of 1943 original) (Louisiana State University Press, Baton Rouge), at pp. 3–6. His parents were Philip Benjamin and Rebecca de Mendes.

[3] A. L. Goodhart, *Five Jewish Lawyers of the Common Law* (1949) (Oxford University Press, London), p. 5.

[4] See, e.g., Meade, *op cit*, at pp. 11–12.

[5] See, D. G. Dalin, *Jewish Justices of the Supreme Court: From Brandeis to Kagan* (2017) (Brandeis University Press, Waltham), at p. 9.

Haven Benjamin "made an excellent record as a scholar ..."[6]. As one of his contemporaries was later to recall, "he easily and without dispute, took at once the highest stand in his class, and was acknowledged to be a riddle and a prodigy of intellectual power"[7]. He was seemingly a popular student[8] and took full advantage of a range of other opportunities which Yale afforded to its undergraduate intake including debating and public speaking.[9]

In late 1827, however, Benjamin suddenly, and "under cloudy circumstances"[10] left the university without graduating. As Curran has noted: "The circumstances of his departure were to haunt him for the rest of his life in America, and they are still obscure"[11]. The rumours over time ranged from "ungentlemanly conduct" to "card playing and gambling", and, in the early months of 1861 following Southern secession, to dishonesty in the form of theft from fellow students.[12] At that time Benjamin, then the Attorney General of the Confederacy, reacted with outrage to this latter suggestion. He informed his friend, James A. Bayard, Jr, that: "I left college in the fall of 1827, in consequence of my father's reverses rendering him unable to maintain me there any longer"[13]

While the historical record is incomplete, some of the

---

[6] A. P. Stokes, *Memorials of Eminent Yale Men* (1914) (Yale University Press, New Haven), Vol. II, p. 261.

[7] "Judah P. Benjamin: His Meteoric Course at Yale – Why he Released a Widow's Son", *New York Times*, 11 May 1884, p. 4.

[8] See, "Judah P. Benjamin's Guardian", *New York Times*, 26 February 1883, at p. 3.

[9] See, e.g., *supra*, note 2, at pp. 23–24, and *supra*, note 6, at pp. 261–262.

[10] R. B. Ginsburg, "From Benjamin to Brandeis to Breyer: Is there a Jewish Seat?" (2002) *Brandeis Law Journal*, Vol. 41, p. 229, at p. 231.

[11] C. Curran, "The Three Lives of Judah P. Benjamin" (1967) *History Today*, Vol. 17, p. 583, at p. 584.

[12] See, e.g., Meade, *supra*, note 2, at pp. 24–30.

[13] Benjamin to Bayard, 19 March 1861. From the original held in the Bayard Papers, Delaware Historical Society, Wilmington; Folder 55: J. P. Benjamin correspondence, 1856–1898. Text kindly supplied by E. Richi, Curator of Printed Materials. See also, *supra*, note 2, at p. 26.

above explanations are inconsistent with the terms of the letter Benjamin himself wrote to the Reverend Jeremiah Day, then President of Yale, on 14 January 1828. It reads in full thus:

It is with shame and diffidence that I now address you to solicit your forgiveness and interference with the Faculty in my behalf. And I beseech you, Sir, not to attribute my improper conduct to any design or intentional violation of the laws of college, nor to suppose that I would be guilty of any premediated disrespect to yourself or any member of the Faculty. And I think, Sir, you will not consider it improper for me to express my hopes, that my previous conduct in college was such as will not render it too presumptuous in me to hope that it will make a favorable impression upon yourself and the Faculty.

Allow me, Sir, here also to express my gratitude to the Faculty for their kind indulgence to my father in regard to pecuniary affairs; and also to yourself and every individual member of the Faculty for their attention and paternal care of me, during the time I had the honor to be a member of the institution.

With hopes of yet completing my education under your auspices, I remain, Sir, your most respectful and obedient servant

J P Benjamin

P.S. May I solicit, Sir, (if not too troublesome to you) the favour of a few lines in answer to this letter, that I may be able to judge of the possibility of my return to the University?[14]

---

[14] Reproduced by Stokes, *supra*, note 6, at pp. 262–263.

Firstly, the text sits uneasily with the theory of "dishonesty" which circulated in 1861 and to which Benjamin had taken such exception. As Goodhart has remarked: "It would be odd indeed to speak of dishonesty as 'disrespect'"[15]. Second, the letter seems at variance with Benjamin's own explanation, noted above, that his departure was occasioned solely by the financial reverses suffered by his father. Though this is referred to in the letter, it is treated both in passing and, in a structural sense, separately from his more detailed apology for his "improper conduct". As Stokes, who uncovered the letter in Yale's *Papers relating to College Discipline, 1821–1830*, has concluded, it "clearly shows that he had committed some serious offense against the government of College".[16] It is also evident that Benjamin was not free, without more, to resume his studies. The irresistible inference is that he had been expelled.[17] There is no evidence that President Day ever responded to Benjamin's plea for reconsideration or that he ever raised the matter with the Faculty.[18] His fate in New Haven was thus sealed.

Though a serious setback, Benjamin was not cowed and did not for long remain with his family in Charleston. Rather, with the confidence so often associated with youth, he soon decided to seek to make a life for himself in New Orleans. This was to prove to be a wise choice.[19] As Rosen has explained: "New Orleans in 1828 was booming. Purchased by the United States in 1803, Louisiana was still very much a multinational and multicultural state. The population was exploding, shipping, trade, and sugar

---

[15] *Supra*, note 3, at p. 5.

[16] *Supra*, note 6, at p. 262.

[17] See, e.g., Dalin, *supra*, note 5, at p. 9, and K. F. Stone, *The Jews of Capitol Hill*, (2011) (Sacrarecrow Press, Toronto), at p. 16.

[18] See, e.g., Stokes, *supra*, note 6, at p. 263.

[19] See, e.g., H. C. Horton, "Judah P. Benjamin: Lawyer under Three Flags", (1965) *American Bar Association Journal*, Vol. 51, p. 1149, at p. 1149.

production were rapidly expanding. It was a place where a young Jewish man with talent and determination could succeed."[20]

Upon his arrival in the city, he was without either financial means or family support. He took various jobs to sustain himself, eventually finding work with a notary public.[21] There he commenced a two-year apprenticeship with a view to being called to the Louisiana Bar. Fortunately for Benjamin access to the profession was not restricted to graduates so long as such a candidate could demonstrate that he or she had received a good classical education. His years at Yale were thus to prove to be of some immediate practical utility. Beyond that, the requirements were few and the curriculum to be followed by candidates, prior to the reforms of 1840, was not standardised. As Gaspard reminds us: "During this time opportunities seemed endless, regardless of a prospective attorney's background or preparation. There were few rules to control admission to the bar, and the question of what constituted adequate training was left open."[22]

At this time Benjamin also acted, on an ad hoc basis, as a private English tutor to the children of elite French families in the city.[23] One such was a teenager by the name of Natalie St Martin, whose parents "were wealthy

---

[20] R. N. Rosen, *The Jewish Confederates* (2000) (University of South Carolina Press, Columbia SC), p. 57.

[21] See, e.g., J. Best, "Judah P. Benjamin: 'That Little Jew from New Orleans'", (2011) *Supreme Court Historical Society Quarterly*, Vol. XXXIII, No.2, p. 6, at p. 7.

[22] E. Gaspard, "The Rise of the Louisiana Bar: The Early Period, 1813–1839" (1987) *Louisiana History: The Journal of the Louisiana Historical Association*, Vol. 28, No.2, p. 183, at p. 183. For a discussion of the nature and significance of the 1840 reforms see, W. M. Billings, "The Supreme Court and the Education of Louisiana Lawyers" (1985) *Louisiana Bar Journal*, Vol. 33, No.2, pp. 75–78. This matter is discussed further in Chapter 5 below.

[23] See, e.g., P. Butler, "Judah P. Benjamin", in W. D. Lewis (ed) *Great American Lawyers*, (1909) (John C. Winston Co, Philadelphia), Vol. VI, p. 257, at p. 260.

and prominent within the powerful French-speaking community".[24] They became engaged and were married on 16 February 1833 in St Louis Cathedral in New Orleans. He was 21; his bride 16 years of age. A marriage contract had been concluded earlier in the same month. Under its terms, a dowry was to be paid consisting of two young "mulatress" slaves and the sum of $3,000.[25] This union, which was to be both highly unorthodox and somewhat controversial,[26] was to subsist until Benjamin's death more than 50 years later.

Some two months earlier, he had been called to the Bar.[27] The young couple continued to live with Natalie's parents; first on Condé Street and thereafter in a mansion on Bourbon Street in the French Quarter.[28] From this comfortable domestic base, Benjamin launched himself into his career in the law. As Butler has remarked "Where there is much commerce there will also be much litigation. And, whether from preference or because he foresaw that this would be the most promising field, it was to commercial law especially that Benjamin devoted himself."[29]

Success was not long in coming; his rise within the Louisiana profession being variously described as

---

[24] C. MacMillan, "Judah Benjamin: Marginalized Outsider or Admitted Insider?" (2015) *Journal of Law and Society*, Vol. 42, p. 150, at p. 156.

[25] See, W. de Ville, The Marriage Contract of Judah P. Benjamin and Natalie St Martin, 1833, (1996) *Louisiana History: The Journal of the Louisiana Historical Association*, Vol. 37, No.1, p. 81, at p. 83. The cash sum was not inconsiderable. One Consumer Price Index inflation calculator estimates its value at approximately $92,000 in 2019 terms.

[26] Much of the general biographical literature on Benjamin contains coverage of this issue and tends to treat his wife in rather unflattering terms. As a general proposition the nature of their relationship lies beyond the scope of this study. For a work of fiction inspired by this unusual union, see V. Delmar, *Beloved* (1956) (Harcourt, Brace & Co, New York).

[27] See, e.g., Meade, *op cit*, at p. 33.

[28] See, *id*, at p. 35. While the Bourbon Street mansion still stands it has fallen on hard times. At the time of writing, it was a venue for exotic dancers.

[29] *Supra*, note 23, p. 265.

"remarkably rapid",[30] "outstanding"[31] and dizzying[32]. As Chief Justice Bermudez of Louisiana was to remark half a century after Benjamin's call: "He did not rise gradually, but at once leaped to distinction among the foremost in the profession. His practice was extensive, substantial and lucrative".[33]

This transformation in his circumstances was due, in no small measure, to his first foray into the then gradually maturing world of Louisiana legal scholarship. In conjunction with Thomas Slidell, a Yale graduate four years his senior,[34] Benjamin published in 1834 a reference work for legal practitioners. Entitled *Digest of the Reported Decisions of the Superior Court of the Late Territory of Orleans, and of the Supreme Court of the State of Louisiana*, it was very well received and afforded its authors greatly enhanced visibility within the local legal profession.[35] As US Supreme Court Justice Ruth Bader Ginsburg has remarked: "it treated comprehensively for the first time Louisiana's uniquely cosmopolitan and complex legal system, derived from Roman, Spanish, French, and English sources".[36]

---

[30] M. J. Kohler, "Judah P. Benjamin: Statesman and Jurist" (1904) *Publications of the American Jewish Historical Society*, No. 12, p. 63, at p. 69.

[31] Goodhart, *supra*, note 3, at p. 6.

[32] See, Dalin, *supra*, note 17, p. 9.

[33] "In Memoriam" (1884) *Reports in the Supreme Court of Louisiana*, Vol. 36, p. vi.

[34] Later an Associate Justice of the Supreme Court of Louisiana and eventually Chief Justice of the state.

[35] (1834) (J F. Carter, New Orleans). In the view of Stone, *supra*, note 17, at p. 17: "Benjamin and Slidell's legal casebook proved to be an immediate success. It permitted the twenty-three-year-old attorney to enter doors that otherwise would have been firmly locked and barred. Almost overnight, he acquired a measure of *gravitas* that men twice his age could never hope to attain."

[36] *Supra*, note 10, p. 231. As MacMillan, *supra*, note 24, p. 158 has explained: "the observations were more in the nature of brief rules arranged alphabetically than principles supported by reason or precedent and arranged within a coherent thesis". It was thus less intellectually ambitious or as impressive in scholarly terms as his treatise on the law of sale written in England in the late 1860s and discussed in Chapters 4 and 5 of this study.

In the language of modern comparative law scholarship, Louisiana is very much an example of a mixed legal system.[37] A revised version of this book was produced by Slidell alone in 1840 Benjamin by that time being fully occupied with the demands of clients.

As Butler has noted: " within ten years of beginning practice [Benjamin] was not only a recognized leader at the bar but so securely established financially that he could begin to turn his attention to things other than law".[38] One such enthusiasm was elective politics, and in this sphere, he was also to enjoy considerable success. In the words of Rosen:

> Benjamin climbed the political ladder the old-fashioned way as campaign worker, manager, lawyer, and finally as a candidate for office. ... He was elected to the Louisiana House of Representatives from New Orleans in 1842 and was an active participant in the constitutional conventions of 1844–45 and 1852 called to rewrite the state constitution. His brilliant performance at the 1852 constitutional convention won him many supporters and he was elected to the Louisiana Senate as a Whig that same year.[39]

That said it continued to be "at times consulted with great profit" for many years. See, *supra*, note 33, at p. vi.

[37] See, e.g., V. V. Palmer, "Mixed Legal Systems", in M. Bussani and U. Mattei (eds), *The Cambridge Companion to Comparative Law* (2012) (Cambridge University Press, Cambridge), at pp. 368–383. In particular, it falls within the "mixed jurisdiction" branch of that area of scholarship the focus of which is on those systems which manifest a mix of civil law and common law influences. See generally, V. V. Palmer, *Mixed Jurisdictions Worldwide: The Third Legal Family* (2012, 2nd ed.) (Cambridge University Press, Cambridge).

[38] *Supra*, note 23, p. 266.

[39] *Supra*, note 20, p. 58. This was a common path. As Gaspard, *supra*, note 22, remarked at p. 192 of her study of the state Bar between 1813 and 1839: "Almost half of the lawyers held political office. By holding political office, an attorney served his community and furthered his career at the same time."

Not content with two demanding careers operating in tandem, Benjamin, in the early 1840s, decided to add a third by becoming the part-owner of a sugar plantation located on the Mississippi in the Parish of Plaquemine some sixteen miles below New Orleans. Through the purchase of "Bellechasse" Benjamin both joined the plantocracy and became a substantial slave owner.[40] In 1843 he also became a father with the birth of a daughter, named Ninette, his only child.

While these developments brought their own demands, he did not abandon his career in the law which was becoming increasingly focused: "[h]e preferred appeals to ordinary cases and judges to juries".[41] In this period, one case, in particular, proved to be of national interest;[42] namely, *Thomas McCargo v New Orleans Insurance Company*[43] decided by the Supreme Court of Louisiana in March 1845. As with the *Keyn* case some thirty years later, while in English exile,[44] it was the underlying facts which commanded the attention of the public. Here they revolved around an audacious effort at self-emancipation at sea. In brief, in late October 1841 an American merchant vessel, the brig *Creole*, embarked at various places in the State of Virginia, some 135 enslaved persons for transportation to New Orleans. Both were so-called slave states. While by this time, the United States had abolished the international slave trade this was an intra-American voyage which was not prohibited in law. As Moore reminds us: "On the night of the 7th of November a portion of the slaves revolted, wounded the master, chief mate, and two of the crew,

---

[40] See, e.g., E. N. Evans, *Judah P. Benjamin: The Jewish Confederate* (1988) (Free Press, New York), pp. 32–33.

[41] T. Wortham, "BENJAMIN, Judah Philip", *American National Biography* (1999) (Oxford University Press, New York), Vol. 2, p. 568, at p. 569.

[42] As to which see, e.g., Evans, *op cit*, pp. 37–39; and Butler, *supra*, note 23, at pp. 268–269.

[43] 10 Rob.(LA) 202 (1845).

[44] Discussed in Chapter 4 of this study in some detail.

and murdered one of the passengers, and having secured possession of the vessel, ordered the mate, under pain of death, to steer for Nassau, where the brig arrived on the 9th of November".[45]

The destination selected was not a case of mere happenstance. Nassau was the capital of the then British colony of the Bahamas lying to the east of the Florida coast. Britain had abolished slavery within the Empire by Act of Parliament in 1833, and this legislation had entered into force the following August.[46] In evidence for the Louisiana courts, taken under commission in April 1842, George Campbell Anderson, the Attorney General of the colony, summarised the resulting legal position in the Bahamas in these words:

> . . . as slavery is abolished throughout the British dominions, the moment a vessel comes into a British port with slaves on board, to whatever nation such vessels may belong, and however imperious the necessity may have been which drove her into such port, such slaves became immediately entitled to the protection of British laws, and that the right of their owners to treat and deal with them as slaves, ceases.[47]

In the *Creole* case, however, emancipation did not prove to be automatic. The colonial authorities first made enquiries as to the identity of those who had been directly involved in the insurrection which had, as noted above, resulted in both injury and death. A total of nineteen persons, all slaves, were deemed to be so implicated. These were separated from the rest and detained in Nassau "until reference could be made to the [British] Secretary of

---

[45] J. B. Moore, *A Digest of International Law* (1906) (Government Printing Office, Washington, DC), Vol. II, p. 351.

[46] See, *id*, p. 352.

[47] *Supra*, note 43, p. 251.

State, to ascertain whether the parties detained should be delivered over to the American government, or not; and, if not, how otherwise to be disposed of".[48] Thereafter all but five slaves, who elected to remain on board, went ashore – notwithstanding the diplomatic protests of the American Consul – and thus became free. Many left for the British West Indian colony of Jamaica in the following days,[49] the remainder blending into the local population. On or about 18 November the *Creole* departed Nassau en route to New Orleans.

This incident "gave rise to animated discussions in the British Parliament as well as in the Congress of the United States, and came near breaking up the negotiations between Mr Webster and Lord Ashburton in 1842"[50]. These diplomatic discussions embraced several important and sensitive matters between the USA and the UK and in particular a range of issues relating to the delimitation of the border between America and what is now Canada (then British North America). Fortunately, these talks were not derailed and were brought to a conclusion in the Treaty of Washington of 9 August of that year. In addition to addressing international frontier and related questions, the Treaty also made provision for certain unrelated matters of common interest including, *inter alia*, initiatives to suppress further the international slave trade (Articles VIII and IX) and to establish bilateral extradition arrangements between the two countries (Article X). As will be seen in Chapter 3 of this study, the limited reach of the latter was to prove to be of value to Benjamin upon his flight into English exile in 1865.

---

[48] *Id*, p. 319. Two members of this group died in detention. The remaining seventeen were eventually released by order of the Court of Admiralty of the colony for want of jurisdiction over the offences in question. See, *id*, at p. 250.

[49] See, *id*, at p. 232.

[50] *Supra*, note 45, p. 352.

At a more parochial level, the slave owners called upon their insurers to indemnify them against loss. One such was Thomas McCargo who claimed in respect of the loss of twenty-six slaves valued at $800 each. The New Orleans Insurance Company denied liability. McCargo sued, and the Commercial Court issued judgment in his favour for $18,400.[51]

The insurance company appealed. For this purpose, it retained Benjamin (somewhat ironically given his status as a slave owner and planter), his friend and co-author Thomas Slidell, and one F. B. Conrad. The case was "elaborately argued by brief and *viva voce*"[52] in the summer of 1844 and judgment was delivered by Justice Henry A. Bullard[53] of the state Supreme Court in March 1845. As the Judge noted, several actions had been raised against various New Orleans insurers: "As all the cases relate to the same voyage, and all the slaves insured were lost at the same time and by the same disaster, they have all been considered together; and it is supposed that the opinion which we are about to pronounce in one of the cases, will be decisive for all."[54]

The arguments presented by Benjamin and his co-counsel were both wide-ranging and scholarly. They covered several critical issues of insurance law, including

---

[51] *Supra*, note 43, p. 258. A note to the Supreme Court judgment clarifies the basis for the award thus: "The amount sued for was $20,800. The jury deducted $800 for one of the slaves who reached New Orleans in safety. A further sum of $1,600 appears to have been deducted, as half of the value of four of plaintiff's slaves, who were proved to have taken part in the insurrection, the jury being of opinion that their loss should be divided between the insurers and the plaintiff."

[52] *Id*, p. 312.

[53] Bullard was a graduate of Harvard and a Judge of the Louisiana Supreme Court from 1834 to 1846. In the following year he was appointed Professor of Civil Law in the Law School of Louisiana. See, e.g., D. J. Bonquois, "The Career of Henry Adams Bullard, Louisiana Jurist, Legislator and Educator" (1940) *Louisiana Historical Quarterly*, Vol. 23, p. 999 *et seq*.

[54] *Supra*, note 43, p. 312.

that of "proximate cause", as well as the domestic and international law relating to slavery, and various relevant doctrines of the international law of the sea.[55] The arguments are replete not only with references to the Civil Code of Louisiana, to statute and case law, but to doctrines of Roman law, and to French, Spanish and other authorities. Benjamin's treatment of slavery issues was regarded as unusually frank and sensitive by the standards of the day. By way of illustration, one of the lines of argument pressed by counsel for the insurers was that they had been, in law, discharged, the vessel having been rendered unseaworthy by virtue, *inter alia*, of overcrowding.[56] There being no federal legislation directly applicable to a slave cargo the point was argued by analogy from an Act of Congress of 1819 regulating the matter in respect of "ordinary passengers". Had it applied the maximum number would have been sixty-three. In the case of the *Creole* 135 slaves had been embarked. The argument was advanced thus:

> Now this Act of Congress was based upon considerations of humanity, and it was deemed necessary to enact such a law, although our country has always been disposed to encourage the immigration of foreigners. Will this court be disposed to recognize one standard of humanity for the white man, and another for the negro? Will any reasonable man say that 135 negroes would be as cheerful, contented and indisposed to insurrection, under such circumstances of discomfort, as they would have been in a larger and more commodious vessel?[57]

At a later stage and on a different head of argument, it was directly put to the court "that slavery is a contravention of the law of nature, is established by the concurrent

---

[55] See, *id*, at pp. 259–286.
[56] See, *id*, at p. 259.
[57] *Id*, p. 260.

authority of writers on national law, and of adjudications of courts, from the era of Justinian to the present day".[58] In the course of addressing the nature of the responsibility of the Bahamian colonial authorities counsel urged the following view of international law:

> [D]oes the law of nations make it the duty of Great Britain to refuse a refuge in her dominions to fugitives from this country, whether black or white, free or slaves? It would require great hardihood to maintain the affirmative as to whites, but the color of the fugitive can make no possible difference. It will scarcely be pretended that the presumption of our municipal law that blacks are slaves, is to be made a rule of the law of nations; and, if not, in what manner are the British authorities to determine between the blacks and whites reaching their ports on the same vessel, the former asserting their liberty, and the latter denying the fact, and claiming the blacks as slaves?[59]

These and other kindred lines of argument advanced on behalf of the insurers were by no means commonplace in Louisiana or the Deep South in the 1840s. It is not surprising, therefore, though it is deeply ironic, that Butler informs us that Benjamin's brief "was printed in pamphlet form and widely circulated".[60]

The terms of the policy in question exempted the insurers from "any liability on account of losses which might be sustained in consequence of a mutiny, or insurrection on board; they assuming all other risks, and particularly restraints, arrests, and detentions by foreign powers, or the emancipation of the slaves by foreign interference".[61]

---

[58] *Id*, p. 279.
[59] *Id*, p. 283.
[60] *Supra*, note 23, p. 269.
[61] *Supra*, note 43, p. 314.

To Bullard, J. the critical question was "whether the loss of the slaves was caused by the insurrection, or by illegal and unauthorised interference on the part of the authorities of Nassau".[62] Following a detailed consideration of the facts, it was concluded "that the insurrection of the slaves was the cause of breaking up the voyage, and prevented that part of the cargo, which consisted of slaves, from reaching the port of New Orleans; and, consequently, that the defendants are not liable on the policy in this case".[63] The judgment of the Commercial Court was reversed; "ours is for the defendants, with costs in both courts".[64]

It is of interest to note that while this, in effect, brought domestic proceedings to a close, the US government remained much engaged with the matter at the diplomatic level. Its firm view was that, as a matter of international law, ships driven into foreign ports or internal waters by *force majeure* or distress must be afforded an enhanced degree of immunity from the jurisdiction of the coastal state. In this instance, it was asserted that the British colonial authorities had failed in their duty to afford the American vessel and its "cargo" the requisite level of protection.

In *McCargo* Bullard had prudently declined to judge whether the facts of the *Creole* incident might properly give rise to a state-to-state claim.[65] In the early 1850s several somewhat similar maritime cases,[66] including the *Creole*, were submitted to a form of international dispute settlement[67] by the US and UK governments. The

---

[62] *Id.*

[63] *Id*, p. 332.

[64] *Id.*

[65] See, *id*, at p. 327.

[66] In the case of the *Enterprise* in February 1835 a US vessel with slaves aboard put into the British colony of Bermuda; in that of the *Hermosa* in October 1840 the vessel was wrecked off the island of Abaco in the Bahamas. In both instances the slaves were freed by operation of colonial law and authority.

[67] In the form of a mixed claims commission.

Commissioners being divided, the issue was referred to the Umpire for final determination. Bates, the Umpire, held in favour of the United States position[68] in respect of the *Creole* and awarded compensation to the slave owners and associated claimants in the sum of $110,330.[69] In so doing, he remarked:

> These rights, sanctioned by the law of nations – *viz*: the right to navigate the ocean, and to seek shelter in the case of distress or other unavoidable circumstances, and to retain over the ship, her cargo, and passengers, the laws of her own country – must be respected by all nations . . .".[70]

This determination was seen to flow from the Umpire's then relatively uncontroversial – though now quite shocking – conclusion as to the status of the institution of slavery in the public international law of the mid-nineteenth century. In his words:

> I need not refer to authorities to show that slavery, however odious and contrary to the principles of justice and humanity, may be established by law in any country; and, having been so established in many countries, it can not be contrary to the law of nations.[71]

---

[68] See, *'Brig Creole'* (USA v Great Britain) XXIX Reports of International Arbitral Awards, p. 26, at pp. 51–53.

[69] See, Moore, *supra*, note 45, at p. 361. This included an award to "William H. Goodwin, for self and Thomas McCargo" of $23,140. See, E. Hornby (ed.) *Report of the proceedings of the Mixed Commission on Private Claims, established under the convention between Great Britain and the United States of America, of 8 February, 1853: with the judgments of the commissioners and umpire* (1856) (Harrison and Sons, London), p. 376, at p. 393.

[70] *Supra*, note 68, p. 53.

[71] In the view of R. R. Churchill and A V. Lowe, *The Law of the Sea* (3rd ed: 1999) (Manchester University Press, Manchester), p. 68, "it is most unlikely that the monstrous illegality of slavery would today be considered to be protected by the essentially humanitarian distress rule". To the same effect, see, e.g., J. E. Noyes, Ships in Distress, in *Max Planck Encyclopedia of Public International Law* (on-line edition), at para 24.

The acquisition of the Bellechasse plantation provided Benjamin with an opportunity to re-centre his social base. Though he continued his professional activities from offices in the city, the plantation became the focus of his family and social life. This domestic reorientation, however, did not commend itself to his wife. In the summer of 1845, she and her daughter relocated to France.[72] Save for a brief period in the late 1850s they would never live in America again. While then, as now, such a move was highly unusual, it did not result in divorce. Benjamin continued to provide them with financial support and retained contact through what would become annual visits to Europe until these were interrupted by the outbreak of the Civil War.

Benjamin continued with and deepened his interest in the plantation in the years which followed. In 1847 he "invited his mother, his widowed sister, Mrs Rebecca Levy, and her young daughter to come to Louisiana and live at Bellechasse".[73] The plantation house was rebuilt in a grand style, and Benjamin devoted more and more of his time to the improvement of its sugar cultivation and production. Bellechasse also had a wider significance. In the words of Dalin, it symbolised "Benjamin's acceptance into Louisiana's slave-owning aristocracy, thereby furthering his political career".[74] This too, as noted earlier, was progressing apace though it was increasingly time-consuming. Though he does not appear to have totally

---

[72] See, e.g., Evans, *supra*, note 40, at p. 33; and Meade, *supra*, note 2, at pp. 57–58.

[73] Meade, *op cit*, p. 58.

[74] *Supra*, note 5, p. 9. This was also a well-worn path for the early lawyers of the state. Of the 565 who made up the Louisiana Bar prior to 1840, around 20 per cent are said to have bought plantations either in their home state or in Mississippi. As Gaspard has noted, *supra*, note 22, at pp. 193–194: "One reason for such a choice was the possibility of making more money from sugar, cotton, rice, and slaves. Another was an obvious desire to join the highest social class in the state, the planter elite."

The Confederate Jurist

abandoned his law practice, it was, for a period, much de-emphasised.

In the latter half of the 1840s Benjamin's horizons progressively lifted beyond the confines of Louisiana. He was, for instance, despatched by the US Federal authorities to California to assist with the difficult issue of land disputes which had arisen following its enforced transfer from Mexican sovereignty.[75] In 1848 he was admitted, in the same term as Abraham Lincoln, to practice before the US Supreme Court.[76] In the same year, as a Presidential elector, "he traveled to Washington for the inauguration of Zachary Taylor, meeting Cabinet members, Senators, and Judges at state dinners and events".[77] It was little wonder that he would invite William C. Micou, a New Orleans attorney, to join his law firm as a partner thus to diminish his professional burden.[78]

Benjamin's political star remained in the ascendant. As noted earlier, in 1852 he had become a member of the State Senate. Not long thereafter political attention turned to the representation of Louisiana in the US Senate in Washington, DC. It will be recalled that prior to the entry into force of the Seventeenth Amendment to the Constitution of the United States in 1913, Senators were elected by state legislatures and not directly by popular vote. Benjamin emerged as a candidate, in the words of Rosen, "[a]t the right place at the right time – and with the right connections – Benjamin was elected . . .".[79]

However, serious financial challenges had arisen in relation to his interest in the Bellechasse plantation. The first came in the form of severe damage to crops and land

---

[75] See, e.g., Meade, *op cit*, at pp. 64–65. See also Stokes, *supra*, note 6, at p. 263.
[76] See, MacMillan, *supra*, note 24, at p. 162.
[77] Evans, *supra*, note 40, p. 41.
[78] See, Meade, *supra*, note 2, at p. 66.
[79] *Supra*, note 20, p. 58.

JUDAH PHILIP BENJAMIN

Figure 1.1 1853 portrait of Benjamin by Adolph Rinck. Reproduced courtesy of The Louisiana Supreme Court Portrait Collection.

resulting from the flooding of the Mississippi River.[80] The second has been described by Meade thus:

> To add to his troubles, a friend failed to meet his financial obligations, so that Benjamin had to pay a $60,000

[80] See, e.g., Butler, *supra*, note 23, at p. 274.

note which, in accordance with the custom of the day, he had generously, but unwisely, endorsed.[81]

The Bellechasse plantation in its entirety – buildings, equipment and 129 slaves – went to auction on Monday 12 January 1852 "in order to effect an amicable partition between the joint owners" – the venue being the opulent Rotunda of the St Louis Hotel in New Orleans said to have inspired scenes in *Uncle Tom's Cabin* published later the same year.[82] Benjamin then purchased a home in the suburbs of New Orleans primarily for the use of those members of his wider family who had become associated with Bellechasse. Thus ended his period as a sugar planter and substantial slave owner.

Though financially diminished, Benjamin was not impecunious. He moved to shared bachelor quarters in New Orleans but continued to socialise in the elite Boston Club. As one commentator has remarked:

Without the usual ties of a married man, Benjamin found relaxation and companionship at his clubs. They also helped to further his career and to set his mind in a conservative mould. Obviously, the members of the Boston Club had the most influence upon him. For reasons of conviction or expediency, they were

---

[81] *Supra*, note 2, p. 90.

[82] An original of the poster advertising the sale is preserved in the manuscripts collection of the National Library of Scotland (shelfmark H. S.632(2)). Of the slaves, twenty-six were children aged 10 or under, fifty-three were men and fifty were women. Several of the adults had identified specialist skills. At least one was disabled. See also, H. B. Stowe, *Uncle Tom's Cabin* (1852)(John Cassell, London). See in particular the illustration of Emmeline about to be sold to the highest bidder opposite p. 290. The link between the Rotunda and the Stowe text is referenced by several sources. See, e.g., M. D. McInnes, *Slaves Waiting for Sale: Abolitionist Art and the Slave Trade* (2011) (University of Chicago Press, Chicago), at pp. 195–196. I am in the debt of Ms D. Petherbridge of the National Library of Scotland for her assistance on this issue.

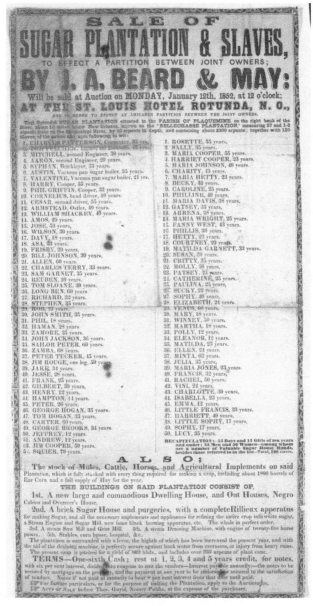

Figure 1.2 Poster advertising the 1852 sale of Benjamin's Plantation and Slaves. Advertisement for "Sale of sugar plantation & slaves", Bellechasse, Louisiana, 1852. [National Library of Scotland shelfmark: H.S.632 (2)] CC BY 4.0.

Figure 1.3 Slave Auction in the Rotunda of the St Louis Hotel, New Orleans. "Sale of estates, pictures and slaves in the Rotunda, New Orleans." Illustration by W. H. Brooke FSA, engraved by J. M. Starling. Plate facing page 335, Vol I, The slave states of America by J. S. Buckingham, 1842. CC BY 4.0.

defenders of the *status quo* and many possessed that pleasant ability (not confined to Southerners) to look at a social abuse and not see it.[83]

He also returned to the practice of law with renewed energy.[84] As Chief Justice Bermudez was to recall in his May 1884 memorial address in the Louisiana Supreme Court, "financial disorders drew him back to the forensic

[83] Meade, *supra*, note 2, p. 83.
[84] See, e.g., Butler, *supra*, note 23, at p. 274.

arena, where he soon recuperated from his losses. To his clients he was infallible".[85] It was within this context that Benjamin prepared for his move to Washington, DC, and it perhaps provides a basis for an understanding of the pivotal career choice which he would soon make.

Prior to taking up his seat in the US Senate in March 1853, Benjamin was unexpectedly offered the opportunity to serve in another, co-equal, branch of American constitutional governance. It is the accepted wisdom of his biographers[86] – reinforced by other commentators[87] including numerous legal historians[88] – that, in the dying weeks of his Presidency in early 1853, Millard Fillmore offered him nomination to the US Supreme Court – an honour he declined. Perhaps unsurprisingly, given that no formal process of nomination was ever initiated, there is scant hard and direct historical evidence for this view. However, the circumstantial evidence supporting this theory is relatively strong. The context was provided by the death of Justice John McKinley of Alabama in the summer of 1852. There was a strong sentiment that his replacement should also come from the Fifth Circuit then consisting of Alabama and Louisiana.[89] In mid-August Fillmore nominated Edward A. Bradford, a well-respected

---

[85] *Supra*, note 33, p. vi.

[86] See, e.g., Evans, *op cit*, at pp. 83–84; and Meade, *op cit*, at pp. 84–85.

[87] See, e.g., R. Aitken, "The Unusual Judah P. Benjamin" (1996) *Litigation*, Vol. 22, No.3, p. 49, at p. 50. See also, Best, *supra*, note 21, at p. 8, Curran, *supra*, note 11, at pp. 585–586, and Horton, *supra*, note 19, at p. 1158. To the same effect see, *The Times* (London), 5 August 1872, at p. 3.

[88] See, e.g., Goodhart, *supra*, note 3, at p. 7; and MacMillan, *supra*, note 24, at p. 161.

[89] See, e.g., C. B. Swisher, *History of the Supreme Court of the United States: The Taney Period* (1974) (Macmillan Publishing, New York) at p. 240 [being Vol. V of this magisterial history of the court]. In 1849 Congress gave Justice McKinley, who had ties to Louisville, authority to hold court in Kentucky "in the absence of the judge of the Eighth Circuit, to which Kentucky officially belonged." *Id*.

Attorney in New Orleans[90] – and later a partner of Benjamin in that city. As has been pointed out elsewhere, "[t]he Democratic majority in the Senate, looking forward to the election of Franklin Pierce to the Presidency and hoping for a Democratic appointment, failed to act on the nomination".[91]

In the months which followed "many names were discussed for the Supreme Court position, including prominent persons not residing in the circuit of the vacancy".[92] Eventually, on 10 January 1853, the out-going President opted for Senator George E. Badger of North Carolina. Though Badger had the advantage of being a member of the US Senate, his nomination met with stiff opposition from the Democratic majority in that body; opposition which, in the end, he was unable to surmount. Eventually, as Abraham has remarked "Senator Badger . . . saw his nomination permanently 'postponed' by one vote, 25:26".[93]

Although the Badger nomination was in effect killed off on 11 February 1853 and the President was due to demit office on 4 March, he decided to make one final attempt to fill the Supreme Court vacancy. Initially, Benjamin's name was firmly in the frame of media speculation. By way of illustration, on 14 February the *New York Times* wrote: "Mr Benjamin, the new Senator, if nominated would probably be confirmed".[94] The following day the same newspaper reported that "[i]f the President nominates Benjamin for the Supreme Court, the Democrats are determined to

---

[90] See, E. B. Monroe, "BRADFORD, EDWARD ANTHONY", in K. L. Hall *et al.* (eds) *The Oxford Companion to the Supreme Court of the United States* (2nd ed: 2005) (Oxford University Press, New York), at p. 96.

[91] *Supra*, note 89, pp. 240–241.

[92] *Id*, p. 241.

[93] H. J. Abraham, *Justices and Presidents: A Political History of Appointments to the Supreme Court* (3rd ed: 1992) (Oxford University Press, New York), p. 112.

[94] 14 February 1853, p. 4.

confirm him".[95] Yet when Fillmore acted on 24 February, he put forward the name not of Benjamin but that of his somewhat politically and professionally obscure law partner William C. Micou.[96] It is widely believed that this was done at Benjamin's suggestion.[97] Perhaps unsurprisingly the Senate declined to act upon this nomination, and the vacancy fell to the incoming President to fill. Pierce, having first sounded out the members of the Supreme Court, acted swiftly to nominate John A. Campbell of Alabama who was confirmed by the Senate a few days later on 25 March.[98]

In the words of Nelson, "[h]ad Benjamin accepted and been confirmed, he would have been the court's first Jewish Justice 63 years in advance of the 1916 appointment of Louis D Brandeis".[99] Rather Benjamin took the oath of office as a Senator on 4 March 1853 and thus became the second person of Jewish heritage to achieve membership of that body. The distinction of being the first fell to David Levy Yulee who served as a US Senator from Florida from 1845 to 1851 and again from 1855 to 1861. The two men had much in common. Both had been born in the Danish West Indies (Yulee in 1810 in St Thomas, Benjamin in 1811 in neighbouring St Croix). Both had been trained

---

[95] 15 February 1853, p. 4.

[96] See, e.g., C. Warren, *The Supreme Court in United States History* (Revised ed; 1926) (Little, Brown and Co, Boston), Vol. II, p. 245.

[97] See, e.g., E. B. Monroe, MICOU, WILLIAM CHATFIELD, in *supra*, note 90, at p. 633; and, Dalin, *supra*, note 5, at p. 10.

[98] See, e.g., *supra*, note 89, at pp. 242–243; *supra*, note 96, at p. 245; and, *supra*, note 93, at p. 113. On occasion the literature suggests that Benjamin was offered nomination to the Court by Pierce. See, e.g., Butler, *supra*, note 23, at pp. 280–281; and Kohler, *supra*, note 30, at pp. 71–72. The present author has discovered no evidence, direct or indirect, that this was the case. It should be noted that during his Presidency Pierce was in a position to make only one nomination, that of Justice Campbell in 1853.

[99] G. Nelson *et al.*, *Pathways to the US Supreme Court: From Arena to the Monastery* (2013) (Palgrave Macmillan, New York), p. 85.

in the law. Both were "champions of the slave system . . .".[100] Both encountered anti-Semitism throughout their political careers.[101] For Yulee, this was in spite of the fact that he had converted to Christianity. In the case of Benjamin, however, although "he had no public connection to Judaism, and organized religion played no role in his life"[102] he never formally repudiated his faith or sought to conceal his Jewish origins.

In opting for his political career in the Senate, Benjamin perhaps sought the best of both worlds; professional and political. On the one hand, members of the Supreme Court were not, at the time, particularly handsomely paid.[103] On the other, as Goodhart has remarked, Senators in addition to discharging their political duties were "free to engage in private practice so that Benjamin was able to appear in a great number of cases before the United States Supreme Court, especially in those which involved questions of commercial and insurance law".[104] Indeed, the US Supreme Court Reports confirm that he appeared before it as Counsel in every year from 1854 to the secession of Louisiana from the Union in 1861. In the years from 1856 on, and especially in 1860, his participation in Supreme Court proceedings was very frequent indeed. This was no doubt facilitated by the convenient fact that at the time the

---

[100] B. W. Korn, *American Jewry and the Civil War* (2001) (Jewish Publication Society, Philadelphia), p. 19.

[101] See, *id*, at pp. 187–189, and pp. 211–212.

[102] *Supra*, note 20, p. 59.

[103] See, e.g., *supra*, note 89, at p. 243.

[104] *Supra*, note 3, p. 8. See also, e.g., Evans, *op cit*, at pp. 92–93. As MacMillan has noted, he "represented clients from the south, notably Louisiana. The disputes were commercial cases of the sort he had taken in New Orleans: bankruptcy; shipping; estate and succession, and land disputes". *Supra*, note 24, pp. 162–163. For an early but high profile case heard by the Supreme Court, on appeal from the US Circuit Court for the Eastern District of Louisiana, in the December Term 1853 see, *Executors of John McDonogh v Murdoch* 56 US 367 (1854).

court sat in the US Capitol and in that sense was co-located with the US Senate.[105]

Upon his relocation to the nation's capital, Benjamin moved to reinforce his New Orleans law firm by bringing in Edward A. Bradford; a graduate of Yale and product of Harvard Law School. He was also, as noted earlier, an unsuccessful Fillmore nominee to the US Supreme Court.[106] For the remainder of the decade the firm, now known as Benjamin, Bradford and Finney, prospered.

As Meade has pointed out "[a]ssured that the New Orleans practice was in capable hands, Benjamin devoted himself to his political duties, his practice before the United States Supreme Court, and various business projects appearing only occasionally in the Louisiana courts".[107] He did not, however, confine his business or professional activities to Washington, DC. By way of illustration, in the Autumn of 1854 he set sail to Ecuador and thence to the Galapagos Islands to press the land and natural resource claims of one General José Villamil; in particular in the hope and expectation of acquiring valuable guano deposits. The trip lasted several months. Somewhat embarrassingly though the claim prospered "of guano there was none".[108] Benjamin was also involved in various railway development projects both in the United States and in Mexico[109] and to which he devoted much time and energy. The most ambitious of these was a project to connect the Atlantic and the Pacific by rail across the Mexican Isthmus of Tehuantepec[110] which unfortunately

---

[105] The current and imposing home of the court ('the marble palace') was only completed in 1935.

[106] See, e.g., *supra*, note 90. William Micou died in 1854.

[107] *Supra*, note 2, p. 90.

[108] *Id*, p. 97.

[109] See, e.g., Butler, *op cit*, at pp. 276–277.

[110] Discussed in some detail by Meade, *supra*, note 2, at pp. 73–75, and pp. 121–123.

was not brought to fruition by the time of the outbreak of the war of secession.[111]

That he was able to devote so much time and energy to his legal and business interests was due, in part, to the fact that his wife and daughter continued to reside in Paris thus freeing him from the normal demands of family life. In Washington, he lived in shared accommodation in a fashionable neighbourhood with other political figures in what was commonly known as a "mess".[112] He did not, however, entirely neglect his political duties, though his footprint in the Senate, save in respect of the issues of slavery and later secession (discussed in Chapter 2 of this study) was relatively slight. Perhaps his most noted contribution was as a member of the Committee on Private Land Claims. It should be recalled that the Democrats dominated the Senate and thus controlled committee membership. They allocated the most sought after on a partisan basis. Benjamin had been elected as a Whig – a political grouping now in decline. On 2 May 1856, in the midst of a noted debate on slavery (discussed later), he abandoned them and became a Democrat. Thereafter he allied closely with his fellow Louisiana Senator John Slidell who was the brother of his co-author, Thomas, and perhaps the state's most influential Democratic politician of the time.[113]

It was under this new political banner that Benjamin, having turned down the offer of appointment from President Buchanan of the US Ambassadorship to Spain in the summer of 1858,[114] sought re-election to the US Senate.

---

[111] Benjamin appears to have had hopes that the project might revive. When he fled Richmond in 1865 he took with him bonds, stock and other documents detailing his interests in the company. The box containing these items fell into the hands of Union forces. See, e.g., Evans, *op cit*, at p. 93.

[112] See, Meade, *op cit*, at pp. 107–108.

[113] See, e.g., *id*, pp. 98–106.

[114] See, *id*, at pp. 113–114; and Best, *supra*, note 21, p. 8.

Figure 1.4 East Elevation of Decatur House, Washington, DC. Historic American Buildings Survey, Creator, Benjamin H. Latrobe, Owner National Trust For Historic Preservation, White House Historical Association, Kathryn K. Lasdow, Thomas T. Waterman, D. F. Ciango, et al., Jack Boucher, Renee Bieretz, and John O. Bostrop, photographer. Decatur House, National Trust for Historic Preservation, 748 Jackson Place Northwest, Washington, District of Columbia, DC. Washington Washington DC, 1933. Photograph. www.loc.gov/item/dc0085/.

In the face of "a most determined fight against him in the legislature"[115] he squeaked home to the narrowest of victories.[116] He was sworn in for what would turn out to be a highly truncated second term in March 1859.

---

[115] Butler, *op cit*, p. 280.

[116] See, e.g., Meade, *op cit*, at p. 119. Several factors had conspired to make Benjamin's re-election problematic. These included, among others, a strength of feeling that both Senators should not be from New Orleans and, more importantly, Benjamin's controversial involvement in a high profile land claim the outcome of which was favourable to his new political mentor Senator Slidell. See further, Evans, *supra*, note 40, at pp. 101–103.

Benjamin had reached what would prove to be the pinnacle of his political influence and authority in Washington. In preparation for the demands this status might bring, he made a major effort to achieve a new balance and stability to his personal and family life by persuading his wife and daughter to join him there. To this end, he rented Decatur House; then, as now, one of the great mansions of the city. Located on the corner of Jackson Place and H Street in the northwest of the city, it abuts Lafayette Square and overlooks the White House.[117] As Aitken has remarked, "[i]n his enthusiasm, he decorated the elegant, three-storey Decatur House with extravagant European opulence".[118] While Natalie did join him in these lavish new surroundings, she failed to settle.[119] In 1859, within a few months of her arrival, she left again for Paris and never returned to America.

Though Benjamin was seemingly far from amused by this development, he remained loyal. His public reaction was pragmatism personified: "He got rid of Decatur House, auctioned off the furnishings, and set to work again".[120] Unsurprisingly, professional distractions were not hard to find and shortly after his wife's departure he became involved in "a case concerned with the ownership of the New Almaden quicksilver mine in California".[121]

---

[117] At the time of writing it is a property of the US National Trust for Historic Preservation and houses a shop for the White House. A metal plaque affixed to its exterior memorialises the "distinguished men who lived here" including Henry Clay and Martin van Buren. Of Benjamin there is no mention.

[118] *Supra*, note 87, p. 51. One expert on the history of the mansion has observed that Benjamin "furnished the house elegantly to regain his wife, an effort which failed as signalled by her departure for Paris, and Benjamin's for the Confederacy". J. N. Pearce, "Decatur House Furnishings 1818–1967" in H. D. Bullock *et al.* (eds), *Decatur House* (1968) (National Trust for Historic Preservation, Washington, DC), p. 25, at p. 27.

[119] See, e.g., Meade, *supra*, note 2, at pp. 123–126.

[120] Curran, *supra*, note 11, p. 586.

[121] MacMillan, *op cit*, p. 163.

It was to prove to be both highly time consuming and extremely lucrative.

Unusually for Benjamin, the *Castillero* case would require his presence in court in California. He would share the burden of preparation and argument with two other well-known figures on the national stage, Reverdy Johnson and J. J. Crittenden, along with several Californian attorneys. The proceedings commenced before the US District Court in San Francisco in early October 1860. As Swisher has noted:

> The trial covered a period of weeks and delved into innumerable intricate problems of law and conflicting statements of facts, with accusations of forgery and fraud. In San Francisco the case attracted attention comparable to major cases before the Supreme Court in Washington.[122]

Benjamin's arguments before the court concluded on 5 November 1860 – the day before the momentous election of Abraham Lincoln as President – and he sailed from San Francisco the following week.[123] He had been on the west coast since mid-August: "Indeed, he was but slightly concerned with politics from the time he left Washington in June until his return there in December".[124] As the events of the next two months were to demonstrate, the timing of this sabbatical from political leadership and responsibility could hardly have been less propitious, as the country hurtled towards secession and war.

As to the case itself, judgment was handed down in January 1861. As Swisher has recalled, "the Castillero interests won their claim to the immediate vicinity of the

[122] *Supra*, note 89, pp. 791–792.
[123] See, Meade, *op cit*, at p. 129 and p. 132.
[124] *Id*, p. 139.

mine although not to the larger surrounding area, and both parties appealed to the Supreme Court".[125] The case came before it in the December Term of 1862 by which time the clash of arms between the Confederacy and the Union was fully engaged. Benjamin, then a member of the Jefferson Davis Cabinet, was in no position to appear.[126] In the final event, while the Supreme Court was split, the majority found in favour of the US government.[127] This, as events were to transpire, marked the end of Judah P. Benjamin's career in the private practice of law in the United States.[128]

---

[125] *Supra*, note 89, p. 792.

[126] It is said that counsel for the claimants did Benjamin "the signal honor of filing a copy of his brief" with the Supreme Court. Kohler, *supra*, note 30, p. 71.

[127] *US v Castillero* 67 US 17 (1863). His co-counsel in this case was, as noted, Reverdy Johnson with whom he interacted professionally on many occasions during his Washington years. A former US Attorney General (1849–1850) Johnson did not side with the Confederacy. Indeed between 1863 and 1868 he served his home state of Maryland in the US Senate. Thereafter (1868–1869) he was for a short time the US Ambassador to the Court of St James in the early period of Benjamin's exile in London.

[128] It is difficult to disagree with Meade, *op cit.*, at p. 158, that "[w]hen he left Washington and accepted a cabinet position in the new Southern Confederacy, he was at the height of his physical and mental if not his moral powers." His primary contribution as a lawyer during the Civil War came during his brief tenure as the first Attorney General of the new "nation". His formal opinions while in that office are reproduced in R. W. Patrick (ed.), *The Opinions of the Confederate Attorneys General 1861–1865* (1950) (Dennis & Co., Buffalo, NY), at pp. 1–36. See further, Chapter 2 below.

2

Slavery, Secession and Benjamin's Confederate Years

Throughout his period of service in the US Senate, Benjamin assumed, unsurprisingly, the mantle of a defender of Southern interests.[1] To him, and the limited constituency which had elected him to office, the preservation and prosperity of the institution of slavery were deemed to be of existential importance.[2] As Kohler has remarked: "Almost all of Benjamin's important political speeches from his advent in the Senate on, were directly concerned with this question."[3] From them flowed his reputation as a great political orator.[4]

It is widely acknowledged that his lengthy address of 11 March 1858 on the Kansas question[5] "provides the most

---

[1] As one commentator has remarked: "Judah P. Benjamin of Louisiana was regarded as one of the most eloquent defenders of the Southern way of life. Though far from a fanatic, he stood squarely with his Senatorial colleagues every inch of the way that led from Washington to Montgomery and then to Richmond." B. W. Korn, "Jews and Negro Slavery in the Old South, 1789–1865", in J. D. Sarna and A. Mendelsohn (eds), *Jews and the Civil War: A Reader* (2010) (New York University Press, New York), p. 87, at p. 109.

[2] See, e.g., C. Curran, "The Three Lives of Judah P. Benjamin" (1967) *History Today*, Vol. 17, p. 583, at pp. 586–587.

[3] M. J. Kohler, "Judah P. Benjamin: Statesman and Jurist" (1904) *Publications of the American Jewish Historical Society*, No12, p. 63, at p. 73.

[4] See, e.g., *id*, at pp. 74–75.

[5] See, e.g., J. M. McPherson, *Battle Cry of Freedom: The American Civil War*, (1990) (Penguin Books, London), at pp. 145–169. See also, e.g., F. Nickell, Kansas – Nebraska Act, in D. S. Heidler and J. T. Heidler, *Encyclopedia of the American Civil War* (2000) (ABC-CLIO, Santa Barbra, Cal), Vol. 3, at pp. 1101–1102.

comprehensive articulation of his views on slavery".[6] In what, by any measure, was a tour de force he couched his argument (as ever) in the language of the law and the constitution.[7] In it he treated his Senate colleagues to a detailed historical account of the legal status of slavery in England and in the British Empire in the decades – in some instances centuries – prior to the Declaration of Independence of the United States. To this he added his interpretation of the position of France and Spain along with their respective colonial possessions and concluded:

> Thus, Mr President, I say that even if we admit for the moment that by the common law of the nations which colonized this continent, the institution of slavery at the time of our independence, was dying away by the manumissions either gratuitous or for a price of those who held the people as slaves, yet so far as the continent of America was concerned, North and South, there did not breathe a being who did not know that a negro, under the common law of the continent, was merchandise, was property, was a slave, and that he could only extricate himself from that status, stamped upon him by the common law of the country, by positive proof of manumission. No man was bound to show title to his negro slave. The slave was bound to show manumission under which he had acquired his freedom, by the common law of every colony.[8]

---

[6] M. Wiseman, "Judah P. Benjamin and Slavery" (2007) *American Jewish Archives Journal*, Vol. LIX, p. 107, at p. 107.

[7] G. D. Cunningham, "Judah P. Benjamin and Secession" (2013) *American Jewish History*, Vol. 97, No1, p. 1, remarks at p. 9: "Benjamin's emphasis on slavery's legal precedent and constitutional sanction is a hallmark of his public debates". As Curran, *supra*, note 2, remarked at p. 587: "To the abolitionists, all this was chop-logic; a web of words spun by the planters' advocate in order to protect property rights in flesh and blood". The outcome was something of a dialogue of the deaf.

[8] *Congressional Globe, 35th Congress, 1st Session, Senate*, p. 1068.

To Benjamin this provided the necessary context for a proper understanding of the provisions of the American Constitution relevant to the slavery question. In his words:

> Two clauses were put in the Constitution, one to guaranty the South its property – it provided for the return to the southern owner of the slave that was recognized as his property; another clause for the North, to prevent a disturbance of the representative basis by importation of slaves. ... That is all the Constitution says on this subject.[9]

To Benjamin the right of property in slaves was thus both recognised and protected by the Constitution – it was no mere creature of state statutes. Furthermore, such property rights were recognised as projecting beyond the territorial boundaries of the slave states. To him these features fatally undermined what he saw as the foundations of the proposition that the US Congress was constitutionally competent to exclude slavery from the western territories.

Benjamin went on to complete his lengthy and no doubt exhausting address with a detailed defence of both the judgment of the US Supreme Court in the (in)famous *Dred Scott* case and of the integrity of Chief Justice Taney.[10] While this speech, which occupies some seven dense pages of the *Congressional Globe*,[11] was heavy on legal learning it is difficult to resist the conclusion that it was light on the language of compromise. His somewhat gratuitous

---

[9] *Id*. For further insights into Benjamin's view of this matter and its implications for the aspirations of his Northern opponents see, e.g., his address of 25 May 1854 in *Congressional Globe, 33rd Congress, 1st Session, Senate*, Appendix, at pp. 766–768.

[10] See, *supra*, note 8, at pp. 1068–1072. See also, *Scott v Sandford* 60 US 393 (1857). For a brief discussion see, M. S. Davis, Dred Scott Case, in D. S. Heidler and J. T. Heidler (eds), *supra*, note 5, Vol. 2, at p. 617–618.

[11] *Supra*, note 8, at pp. 1065–1072.

references, *inter alia*, to "the spirit of fanaticism",[12] the "sanctimonious holiness" and the "cheap philanthropy"[13] of his opponents was hardly the material of the bridge-builder.

To Benjamin secession of the southern states and the outcome of the debate on the future of slavery were inextricably linked. From as early as 23 February 1855 he publicly contemplated the worst: "every day I am more and more persuaded it [the withdrawal of the South] is becoming inevitable . . .".[14] He returned to the issue of the "logic of secession" in much greater detail the following year. On 2 May 1856, he delivered in the Senate what Cunningham has characterised as "the most momentous speech in his national political career".[15] Again, the Kansas question acted as the catalyst.

On this occasion, Benjamin commenced with the proposition that the time for compromise was over. The South, he asserted, "has no longer any compromises to offer or to accept. She looks to those contained in the Constitution itself. By them she will live; to them she will adhere; and if those provisions which are contained in it shall be violated to her wrong, then she will calmly and resolutely withdraw from a compact, all the obligations of which she is expected scrupulously to fulfill, from all the benefits of which she is ignominiously excluded".[16] The slavery issue was too important politically, socially and economically to permit the aspirations of the North to prevail: "Property, safety, honor – existence itself- depend on the decision of the questions which are now pending . . .".[17] He emphasised, however, that separation must be a last resort. He

---

[12] *Id*, p. 1067.
[13] *Id*, p. 1068.
[14] *Congressional Globe, 33rd Congress, 2nd Session, Senate*, Appendix, p. 220.
[15] Cunningham, *supra*, note 7, p. 11.
[16] *Congressional Globe, 34th Congress, 1st Session*, p. 1092.
[17] *Id*, p. 1094.

was not one who believed "in the possibility of a peaceful disruption of the Union". He warned that if it came to secession "dreadful will be the internecine war that must ensue".[18] Given his view as to its likely consequences, it is no surprise that Benjamin was not to become a leading champion of the break-up of the Union.[19] In that sense he was no "fire-eater" but rather a moderate of sorts; a member of the most conservative group of the so-called cooperationists.[20]

As McPherson reminds us "the harvest of disunion came quickly after the thunderstorm of Lincoln's election";[21] an election which, as noted in Chapter 1 of this work, took place while Benjamin was nearing the end of his lengthy sojourn in California to participate in the *Castillero* case. Given his consequential and protracted absence from the political stage, both state and national, Benjamin was no doubt relieved to be in a position to conclude, in a letter of 9 December 1860 to Samuel L. M. Barlow, that "[t]he prudent and conservative" men of the South were not "able to stem the wild torrent of passion which is carrying everything before it. . . . It is a revolution . . . of the most intense character . . . and it can no more be checked by human effort, for the time, than a prairie fire by a gardener's watering pot".[22]

Within a few days, Benjamin publicly committed to secession by adding his signature to an open address,

---

[18] *Id*, p. 1095.

[19] See, e.g., R. D. Launius, "Judah P. Benjamin, 1811–1884", in *Research Guide to American Historical Biography* (1988) (Beacham Publishing, Washington, DC), Vol. 1, p. 129, at p. 130. Indeed, on 7 November 1860 – the day after the election of Lincoln – Benjamin gave a speech in San Francisco containing many pro-Union sentiments. See, e.g., Meade, *infra*, note 24, at pp. 141–142.

[20] See, e.g., W. Hettle, Cooperationists, in D. S. Heidler and J. T. Heidler (eds), *supra*, note 5, Vol. 1, at pp. 497–498.

[21] McPherson, *supra*, note 5, p. 234.

[22] Quoted, *id*, at p. 237.

supported by a clear majority of Senators and Congressmen from seven of the southern slave states, directed to their respective constituents.[23] It reads in part thus:

> The argument is exhausted. All hope of relief in the Union through the agency of committees, Congressional legislation, or constitutional amendments is extinguished. . . . The Republicans are resolute in the purpose to grant nothing that will or ought to satisfy the South. We are satisfied the honor, safety, and independence of the Southern people [require the organization of] a Southern Confederacy – a result to be obtained only by separate State secession . . .[24]

At that stage, no state had yet taken this step though South Carolina was in the vanguard. It convened the first secession convention in Charleston on 17 December, and it did not take the delegates long to decide unanimously on that course of action. Three days later, they formalised this momentous act by ordinance.[25] On New Year's Eve 1860, Benjamin rose in the US Senate to defend South Carolina's right to proclaim independence in this manner and to warn against efforts "to put her down by force of arms".[26] To Meade this "address was probably the greatest he had ever delivered . . .;"[27] to Evans it was "one of the great speeches in American history".[28] Perhaps fittingly it was delivered before a packed public gallery. All knew that although the issue of the day was the action taken by

[23] See, *id*, at p. 254.
[24] Reproduced in R. D. Meade, *Judah P. Benjamin: Confederate Statesman* (2001 reprint of 1943 original) (Louisiana State University Press, Baton Rouge), at p. 146.
[25] See, e.g., W. C. Davis, *Look Away: A History of the Confederate States of America* (2003) (Free Press, New York), pp. 30–32.
[26] *Congressional Globe, 36th Congress, 2nd Session*, p. 212.
[27] *Supra*, note 24, p. 149.
[28] E. N. Evans, *Judah P. Benjamin: The Jewish Confederate* (1988) (Free Press, New York), p. 109.

South Carolina more would follow. As Benjamin emphasised: "Next week, Mississippi, Alabama, and Florida, will have declared themselves independent; the week after, Georgia; and a little later, Louisiana; soon, very soon, to be followed by Texas and Arkansas."[29] He had no doubt that, in time, other slave states would do likewise.

To Benjamin, all were within their rights to do so, and he shared with the Senate, at some length, the legal reasoning by which he had reached this conclusion. It was, to his mind, a constitutionally proper course of action.[30] It was also now inevitable: "The day for the adjustment has passed".[31] Benjamin expressed the hope that this constitutional parting would be in peace but feared otherwise. His peroration took this form:

> What may be the fate of this horrible contest, no man can tell, none pretend to foresee; but this much I will say: the fortunes of war may be adverse to our arms; you may carry desolation into our peaceful land, and with torch and fire you may set our cities in flames; you may even emulate the atrocities of those who, in the war of the Revolution, hounded on the blood-thirsty savage to attack upon the defenseless frontier; you may, under the protection of your advancing armies, give shelter to the furious fanatics who desire, and profess to desire, nothing more than to add all the horrors of a servile insurrection to the calamities of civil war; you may do all this – and more, too, if more there be – but you never can subjugate us; you never can convert the free sons of the soil into vassals, paying tribute to your power; and you never, never can degrade them to the level of an inferior and servile race. Never! Never![32]

[29] *Supra*, note 26, p. 212.
[30] See generally, *id*, pp. 212–217.
[31] *Id*, p. 217.
[32] *Id*.

The public broke into "disgraceful applause, screams and uproar"[33] and the galleries were promptly ordered cleared. As the *New York Times* reported on its front page the following day: "The scene in the Senate . . . was the most intensely exciting that was ever witnessed in that chamber."[34]

The weeks that followed unfolded politically much as Benjamin had predicted and, towards the end of January, "Louisiana became the fourth state to secede from the union".[35] On 4 February he and fellow Senator John Slidell resigned their seats. His farewell speech was, in comparison with that of 31 December, relatively short and rather more measured. He explained why, notwithstanding the very different manner through which it had come under American sovereignty, he considered that his state had a legal right to follow the secessionist route. Benjamin also placed on record his "conviction that the State of Louisiana has judged and acted well and wisely in this crisis of her destiny".[36] To his "brother Senators, on all sides of this Chamber [he bade] a respectful farewell . . ."[37]

In this manner, Benjamin brought his political and legal careers in Washington to an end and "willingly went out with the Southern tide".[38] He packed up and returned to New Orleans. His stay was, however, to be brief. As events transpired, he was soon called upon to serve in the Confederate Cabinet of President Jefferson Davis. As Rosen has explained: "He made arrangements

---

[33] "The National Crisis", *New York Times*, 1 January 1861, p. 1.

[34] *Id.*

[35] *Supra*, note 6, p. 108.

[36] *Congressional Globe, 36th Congress, 2nd Session*, p. 721.

[37] *Id*, p. 722. On the following day Andrew Johnson launched a blistering rebuttal accusing Benjamin, *inter alia*, of hypocrisy and citing his pro-Union speech of 7 November, cited in note 19 above. See, Meade, *supra*, note 24, at pp. 154–155.

[38] Cunningham, *supra*, note 7, p. 19.

to leave his family, his friends, his law practice, and all of his business interests. He made his last public address in New Orleans on February 22 and left for Montgomery".[39]

It will be recalled that even before Benjamin had resigned his seat and made his farewell speech in the US Senate, delegates from the six states which had by then formalised their separation from the United States, including Louisiana, started to gather in the capital of Alabama to chart the way forward.[40] This Provisional Congress convened on 4 February 1861. Time was of the essence, and it was soon agreed that in the circumstances continuity was the key. To the surprise of many, a provisional constitution for the Confederate States of America was agreed on 8 February. It bore a striking resemblance to that of the country from which they had just separated. Work then commenced in framing a more permanent constitutional covenant which was adopted unanimously on 11 March.[41] It too borrowed freely from the Constitution of the United States. As has been noted elsewhere: "The principal differences were its emphasis on states' rights, protecting slavery, and correcting what were regarded as defects in the processes of government".[42] Though Benjamin was not one of its drafters, he was more than content with the outcome. In a letter of 14 March to his friend, Senator James A. Bayard, Jr of Delaware, he stated: "Is not our Constitution admirable in every sense of the word? Is it not close to perfection? . . . It might have been possible to

---

[39] R. N. Rosen, *The Jewish Confederates* (2000) (University of South Carolina Press, Columbia, SC), p. 12.

[40] See generally, *supra*, note 25, at pp. 48–54.

[41] This was ratified on 29 March 1861 and entered into force on 22 February 1862.

[42] For a brief overview see, D. S. Heidler and J. T. Heidler, Constitution CSA, in D. S. Heidler and J. T. Heidler (eds), *supra*, note 5, Vol. 1, at pp. 488–490. The major provisions relating to slavery were, Art I, s9(1) and (2), and Art IV, s2(3).

reform the old instrument still more, but how soberly and prudently have the amendments been made."[43]

By then Benjamin had assumed office as the first Attorney General of the Confederacy and as such was a member of the Cabinet of President Jefferson Davis.[44] In his memoirs written in 1881 Davis recalled his reasons for doing so: "Benjamin of Louisiana had a very high reputation as a lawyer, and my acquaintance with him in the Senate had impressed me with the lucidity of his intellect, his systematic habits, and capacity for labor."[45] Though the men knew one another they were not friends. Indeed Davis took pride in the fact "that not one of those who formed my first cabinet had borne to me the relation of close personal friendship, or had political claims upon me . . .".[46] His appointment also served the wider political purpose of obtaining an appropriate geographical distribution of Cabinet posts among those states which had met in Montgomery.

As Attorney General, Benjamin was also the head of the Confederate Department of Justice. Its creation was something of an innovation; its US equivalent was not

---

[43] From the original held in the Bayard Papers, Delaware Historical Society, Wilmington: Folder 55, J. P. Benjamin correspondence, 1856–1898.

[44] The provisional executive, including the President, was to be elected by the delegates at Montgomery. Each had to be a "citizen" of one of the few states there represented. This disqualified several strong potential Presidential candidates including John C. Breckinridge of Kentucky who had done well in the Deep South in the US Presidential election the previous year. In the end they selected Davis who had represented Mississippi in the US Senate but was not a delegate to the Montgomery meeting. See generally, W. C. Davis, *op cit*, ch. 3.

[45] J. Davis, *The Rise and Fall of the Confederate Government* (1990 reprint of the 1881 original) (Da Capo Press, New York), Vol. I, pp. 207–209.

[46] *Id*, p. 207. See, Figure 2.1 below: being a group portrait of the Confederate Cabinet including President Jefferson Davis, Vice President Alexander Hamilton Stephens, Attorney General Judah P. Benjamin, Secretary of the Navy Stephen R. Mallory, Secretary of the Treasury C. S. Memminger, Secretary of War Leroy Pope Walker, Postmaster John H. Reagan, and Secretary of State Robert Toombs, seated and standing around table.

Figure 2.1 First Cabinet of the Confederate States at Montgomery, 1861. The Cabinet of the Confederate States at Montgomery from photographs by Whitehurst, of Washington, and Hinton, of Montgomery, Alabama. Confederate States of America, 1861. Photograph. www.loc.gov/item/2002735895/.

formed until after the Civil War in 1870.[47] In the words of Patrick:

> The department consisted of the office of the Attorney General (an assistant was later provided), the patent office, the bureau of public printing, and the legal office. Benjamin's duties as Attorney General included the organization of Confederate courts; representing the government before the Supreme Court, when and if that body should be provided for; general supervision of the court officials and the various divisions in the departments; organization of the territories; and advising the President and executive secretaries.[48]

---

[47] See, e.g., J. G. Randall and D. Donald, *The Civil War and Reconstruction* (2nd ed, 1969) (D. C. Heath & Co, Lexington, Mass), at p. 246.

[48] R. W. Patrick, *Jefferson Davis and his Cabinet* (1944) (Louisiana State University Press, Baton Rouge), pp. 158–159.

For a variety of reasons, both practical and political, the Supreme Court of the Confederacy, mandated by Article III, section 1 of the Constitution, was never brought into being.[49] As a consequence Benjamin "was not overtaxed with work"[50] and he busied himself with assisting the President with tasks unrelated to his Cabinet portfolio.[51] As Rosen has noted, "Benjamin rapidly became a close confidante and political advisor to President Jefferson Davis".[52] Over time he became, in the words of Evans, the President's "alter ego",[53] something facilitated in part by his increasingly close social ties with Mrs Varina Davis, the "First Lady" of the new Republic. His influence was thus far greater in this period than the politically "insignificant office" of Attorney General[54] might imply. Benjamin, of course, also attended Cabinet as a full member and did not refrain from contributing to discussion across the range of issues on its agenda. At its first meeting, for instance, it is said that "Benjamin urged the immediate sale of all

---

[49] See, e.g., D. L. Peterson, *Confederate Cabinet Departments and Secretaries* (2016) (McFarland & Co, Jefferson, NC), at pp. 32–33. Of general interest see, W. R. Robinson Jr., *Justice in Grey: A History of the Judicial System of the Confederate States* (1941) (Harvard University Press, Cambridge, Mass.).

[50] Patrick, *op cit*, at p. 159. During his period of office as Attorney General, he prepared but 13 written Opinions. See, Peterson, *op cit*, at pp. 32–33. These ranged from the contract for the award of a mail route to issues concerning the removal of the seat of government from Alabama to Virginia. Most, however, related to the appointment, rank, and pay of members of the armed forces and like matters.

[51] In the words of one modern commentator: "Though he was only Attorney General, Benjamin had already made himself indispensable to Davis. There was so little for him to do at the newly formed Department of Justice that Benjamin could devote most of his energies to whatever appealed. For the time being, he was acting as the President's grand vizier. He shielded Davis from the place-hunters and took on the burden of sorting through many of the tedious but necessary details of government." A. Foreman, *A World on Fire* (2010) (Allen Lane, London), p. 83.

[52] R. N. Rosen, "Jewish Confederates", in J. D. Sarna and A. Mendelsohn (eds), *supra*, note 1, p. 227, at p. 235.

[53] *Supra*, note 28, p. 153.

[54] *Supra*, note 25, at p. 83.

available cotton and the purchase of arms and munitions in preparation for protracted war. The majority of the cabinet, however, felt either that the North would not fight, or that, if they did, the South would win handily".[55] His proposal did not find support. In the view of Meade, had that advice been followed "the Civil War might have ended differently".[56]

In these early months, his reputation steadily grew. In the words of Schouler: "Contemporaries had said at the outset that Toombs was the brain of this Confederacy; but that title, as events developed, belongs rather to Attorney General Benjamin, the ablest, most versatile, and most constant of all Davis's civil counsellors...."[57] It was thus likely that he would be in line for promotion to one of the more important offices of state should an appropriate vacancy arise.

This was not long in coming. In September 1861 Leroy Walker, who had been in poor health, resigned as Secretary of War and on the 17th of that month the President appointed Benjamin as the Acting Secretary. Though a Department of pivotal importance, Benjamin continued for a period of months to also hold the position of Attorney General.[58] By this stage the conflict had started – Fort Sumter had been attacked in April – and the Union had established an increasingly effective naval blockade of Southern ports. Politically a greatly expanded Confederacy had moved its capital from Alabama to the city of Richmond in Virginia.

This appointment seems in retrospect to have been far from inspired. Benjamin, unlike his President, had no

---

[55] H. C. Horton, "Judah P. Benjamin: Lawyer under Three Flags" (1965) *American Bar Association Journal* Vol. 51, p. 1149, at p. 1151.

[56] R. D. Meade, *op cit*, p. 166.

[57] J. Schouler, *History of the United States of America under the Constitution* (1899) (Dodd, Mead & Co, New York), Vol. VI, p. 89.

[58] See, e.g., *supra*, note 48 at pp. 162–163.

military background of any kind. His elevation perhaps says as much about the views of Jefferson Davis as to the nature and extent of his role as Commander-in-Chief as it does about the attributes of Benjamin as trusted counsellor and competent administrator. The resulting working relationship between the two has been described as follows: "The President controlled where military planning was concerned, although he and Benjamin worked out the plans together. The Secretary had virtually a free hand in the business management of the department."[59]

Benjamin, whose appointment was rendered permanent by the Confederate Congress in late November,[60] set about securing improvements in the situation he had inherited. He swiftly "systematized the operations of the department. He delegated, assigned specific tasks to others, and ensured that other people handled the routine matters",[61] thus allowing him to focus on issues of greater importance. These were many and varied. Of them perhaps the most pressing was the need to increase the availability of critical war materials – from guns to gunpowder – by a combination of stimulating domestic production and increasing purchases from abroad. Neither proved to be easy though some progress was recorded during his tenure.[62] A further significant and equally intractable problem was how best to engineer a radical shift in the balance between short-term enlistment to the Confederate armed forces towards securing substantially more long-term volunteers.[63]

Benjamin's efforts to address those and other issues of direct relevance to the war effort were somewhat

---

[59] *Id.* p. 176.
[60] See, e.g., T. Wortham, "BENJAMIN, Judah Philip", in *American National Biography* (1999) (Oxford University Press, New York), Vol. 2, p. 568, at p. 569. Benjamin demitted office as Attorney General at this time.
[61] *Supra*, note 49, p. 140.
[62] See, Patrick, *op cit*, at pp. 164–166.
[63] See, e.g., *id*, at p. 165 and p. 179.

undermined by an uncharacteristic lack of tact and insight in his dealings with Confederate military commanders. In a relatively brief period be managed to fall out with a range of senior army officers including Generals Joseph E. Johnston, P. G. T. Beauregard, and Thomas J. ('Stonewall') Jackson. Several of these figures enjoyed broad public approval, and his disagreements with them served to undermine Benjamin's own standing with the public.[64] This was to prove highly problematic in early 1862 when, in the face of Confederate military reverses, the public search began for a scapegoat.

In February of 1862, just as the Confederacy was in the midst of the transition from the provisional to the permanent Constitutional arrangements, it suffered three military setbacks in quick succession. Two were in the west where the fall of Fort Henry on the Tennessee river early in the month was followed but ten days later by the surrender of nearby Fort Donelson on the Cumberland, along with some 12,000 men, to Ulysses S. Grant.[65] Between these two defeats came another much nearer to the capital; namely, the engagement at Roanoke Island, North Carolina and the surrender of its garrison of in excess of 2,500 troops on 8 February.[66]

Following Roanoke, "Benjamin suffered tremendous criticism from throughout the South. Calls for his resignation were universal, as were demands that Davis dismiss Benjamin, should the latter refuse to step down".[67] This drew its strength from the publicly known fact that the commander of the Confederate force, Brigadier General

---

[64] See generally, *id*, at pp. 167–171.

[65] See, e.g., McPherson, *supra*, note 5, at pp. 396–403. A delighted President Lincoln promoted Grant to Major General.

[66] See, *id*, at pp. 372–373. See also, A. C. Downs, Roanoke Island, North Carolina, in D. S. Heidler and J. T. Heidler (eds), *supra*, note 5, Vol. 4, at pp. 1659–1661.

[67] R. Saunders, Benjamin, Judah Philip, in D. S., Heidler and J. T. Heidler (eds), *supra*, note 5, Vol. 1, p. 209, at p. 210.

Figure 2.2 Benjamin in 1862. From the Confederate $2 note.

Wise, had repeatedly called upon the War Department to reinforce his defences, but to no avail. Much of the Southern press turned against Benjamin, as did their readers among the general public and the political class. On Tuesday 4 March while the Confederate House of Representatives was meeting in Secret Session, James S. Moore of Kentucky offered the following measure of censure which was agreed to:

Resolved, That it is the deliberate judgment of this House that the Honourable J P Benjamin, as Secretary of War, has not the confidence of the people of the Confederate States, nor of the Army, to such an extent as to meet the exigencies of the present crisis, and that we must respectfully suggest that his retirement from said office, and the filling of the same with an incumbent in whom the country and the Army have full confidence, is a high military necessity.[68]

This was advice which Davis was reluctant to accept; a posture which flowed in part from his knowledge of the full facts.[69] Of these the most important – which he was unwilling to share openly – was that the Confederacy did not have to hand the war materials and other support which Wise had requested.[70] He was also loath to lose his most trusted civilian counsellor. In the final event, the President decided on an unorthodox way forward. As Rosen reminds us:

Davis did not seek Benjamin's confirmation as secretary of war under the new, permanent constitution, but instead on March 17, 1862, appointed Benjamin secretary of state of the Confederate States of America, a promotion, as one contemporary observed, in 'the very teeth of criticism'.[71]

It was in this context that Benjamin, who by that time was perhaps "the most unpopular and most hated man in the

---

[68] *Journal of the Congress of the Confederate States of America, 1861–1865* (1904) (Government Printing Office, Washington, DC), Vol. V, at p. 57.

[69] See, e.g., R. D. Meade, *op cit*, at pp. 219–229.

[70] See, e.g., H. Jones, *Blue and Gray Diplomacy: A History of Union and Confederate Foreign Relations* (2010) (University of North Carolina Press, Chapel Hill), at p. 117.

[71] *Supra*, note 39, p. 73.

Confederacy", [72] assumed control of the foreign affairs of his embryonic "nation" and became the Secretary of its Cabinet.

It is important to recall that Benjamin was the third Confederate Secretary of State.[73] The broad contours of its foreign policy had thus been determined at an earlier stage and especially during the period of office of Robert Hunter.[74] The central pillars of the approach adopted were to work for foreign intervention, to challenge the efficacy and legality of the naval blockade[75] and, above all, to actively seek recognition.

The first of these goals had nearly come to pass, due to the miscalculation of others, in late 1861. The government in Richmond had determined to send two "Commissioners" to Europe to progress its diplomatic efforts. James M. Mason, a former US Senator from Virginia, was destined for Britain; John Slidell, Benjamin's one-time political mentor and former US Senator for Louisiana, was heading for France. They first evaded the Union blockade. In Cuba, the two envoys and their assistants embarked on the British flag vessel, *Trent*, and sailed for England. Thereafter their vessel was intercepted by a Union warship. It sent a boarding party to the *Trent*, arrested the Confederate representatives, and returned with them to the United States.[76] Britain (joined by France and others) protested what was seen as a serious violation of the international law of the sea: "Ruptures of diplomatic relations, and even

---

[72] The words of Patrick, *op cit*, at p. 180.

[73] William Browne had been Acting Secretary for a very short period in 1862 prior to Benjamin assuming office.

[74] Hunter held office from July 1861 to February 1862. He succeeded Robert Toombs.

[75] For a discussion of the Union blockade from a legal perspective see, S. C. Neff, *Justice in Blue and Gray: A Legal History of the Civil War* (2010) (Harvard University Press, Cambridge Mass), Ch.8.

[76] For an overview see, e.g., H. F. Dubrulle, Trent Affair, in D. S. Heidler and J. T. Heidler (eds), *supra*, note 5, Vol. 4, at pp. 1972–1974.

war, loomed as genuine possibilities".[77] In the final event, the American government blinked first. It released Mason, Slidell and the others and US Secretary of State Seaward proffered an explanation – which the British treated as an apology – for the action taken. The matter was thus closed and war between the UK and US, which would have been much to the advantage of the South, was averted.[78]

Prior to Benjamin's assumption of office, the Confederacy had secured one form of recognition from members of the international community; namely, recognition of belligerency. Britain took this step, which was much resented by the Lincoln administration, in May of 1861, and France did likewise the following month.[79] Others soon followed.[80] With this act, the recognising states became obliged in law to observe neutrality in the struggle. Though welcome, this was not the form of recognition that the Confederacy craved. It was recognition of statehood[81] that was the Holy Grail of its diplomatic efforts. As Neff has explained:

> Careful note should be taken of the contrast between recognition of belligerency and the larger step of recognition of independent statehood. Recognition of belligerency means that, in the eyes of the recognizing state, the contending sides are precisely on a par with one another in the possession and exercise of the full range of *belligerents'* rights. Recognition of statehood, in

[77] Neff, *op cit*, p. 171.

[78] See generally, e.g., M. B. Ferris, *The Trent Affair: A Diplomatic Crisis* (1977) (University of Tennessee Press, Knoxville).

[79] For the respective texts of these declarations, see, F. Deak and P. C. Jessup (eds), *A Collection of Neutrality Laws, Regulations and Treaties of Various Countries* (1939) (Carnegie Endowment for International Peace, Washington, DC), at pp. 161–162, and pp. 590–592.

[80] See, e.g., Neff, *op cit*, at p. 168.

[81] For the detailed views of the writer on the international law relevant to this issue see, W. C. Gilmore, *Newfoundland and Dominion Status* (1988) (Carswell, Toronto), pp. 194–201, and pp. 222–231.

contrast, is an acknowledgement, again by the recognizing state, that the insurgent side is entitled to the full range of *sovereign* rights. A concrete sign of this distinction concerns diplomatic relations. For one state to recognize a community as an independent state amounts, *ipso facto*, to a willingness to enter into formal and official diplomatic relations with that state. The lesser measure of recognition of belligerency, in contrast, does not have this consequence.[82]

It was to the attaining of this goal that Benjamin turned his attentions upon assuming office and the President afforded to him in this, and other matters, a considerable degree of flexibility. The staff of the Department was small in number.[83] Its Chief Clerk was Littleton Washington. He occupied an adjoining office and met with Benjamin each day. In a "Memoir" of the Secretary of State, written in November 1897, he described the working relationship with the President in these words:

I am sure that Mr Benjamin kept Mr Davis advised of all the important operations of the State Department; but its management, its instructions, correspondence and policies were those of its accomplished head. In selections for positions abroad the President, of course, had the final decision.[84]

In his quest for recognition, formal or tacit, Benjamin concentrated on Britain and, in particular, on France. However, his efforts to engineer a "cleavage" between the two on this subject failed.[85] The French would not act

---

[82] Neff, *op cit*, at pp. 168–169.

[83] See, *supra*, note 24, at pp. 245–246.

[84] Reproduced as Appendix A in D. L. Gibboney (ed), *Littleton Washington's Journal* (2001) (Kindle edition).

[85] See, e.g., *supra*, note 48, at pp. 186–187.

alone; the government in London remained unconvinced of the merits of taking such a bold step. In truth, the case for recognition of statehood needed to be made on the battle-fields of America. As Rosen has noted: "After Gettysburg and Vicksburg in the summer of 1863 recognition was not a real option".[86] Notwithstanding these setbacks, the effort continued but to no real effect.

Of course, Confederate foreign policy was not con-fined to this one issue, but the failure to resolve it in a satisfactory manner had a consequential impact on other areas of concern. This flowed from the fact that while its Commissioners and other agents abroad had diplo-matic mandates, they lacked diplomatic status; while they sought direct access to ministers and policymakers in foreign capitals, they generally had to make do with the deploying of indirect influence.[87] The desire to conduct foreign affairs effectively was further hampered by the practical difficulties, deriving both from the technologies of the time and the challenges of the Union blockade, of communicating with officials overseas. In truth, being the minister of foreign affairs of an unrecognised territorial entity distant from the shores of Europe was, objectively, something of a thankless task.

Notwithstanding these disadvantages, the effort con-tinued to be made, and some successes were achieved. Outside of the issue of recognition, the work of the State Department was largely devoted to "acquainting European governments with the state of the struggle, the advantages of free intercourse and exchange of products with the Southern States, the determination of their people to persist in their efforts, and to meeting the charges and misstatements of the federal authorities".[88] At a more

[86] *Supra*, note 39, p. 77.
[87] See, e.g., *supra*, note 2, at p. 588.
[88] *Supra*, note 84.

practical level governments were encouraged to continue to stretch the concept of neutrality in favour of the South; well illustrated by the construction of commerce raiders, such as the *CSS Alabama*, in the shipyards of Europe.[89] The raising of monies in European financial markets, as with the controversial Erlanger loan, was also of importance. As Gentry reminds us, without the funds secured "purchases of arms, supplies, and ships in Europe would have stopped, and Confederate credit would have been ruined".[90]

The Department of State also had a level of involvement in and responsibility for Confederate secret intelligence and related activity.[91] Other elements of this effort were conducted under the auspices of the Secretary of War and the Secretary of the Navy. The President was centrally involved.[92] In so far as Benjamin is concerned, particular attention was paid to his agents based in and operating from Canada.[93]

Important though the issues confronted by his Department were, Benjamin continued to find ample time to consult with, and perform other services for, President Davis much as he had done in his previous Cabinet roles. He remained efficient in the discharge of business and was adept at delegating tasks to his staff.[94] Furthermore, both he and the President had offices in the Customs House in

---

[89] On the resulting post-conflict *Alabama* arbitration between the UK and US see, e.g., *supra*, note 75, at p. 179 *et seq.* For the text of the award of 14 September 1872 see, *'Alabama' Claims* (USA v Great Britain) XXIX Reports of International Arbitral Awards, pp. 125–134.

[90] J. F. Gentry, "A Confederate Success in Europe: The Erlanger Loan" (1970) *Journal of Southern History*, Vol. 36, No2, p. 157, at p. 157.

[91] See, e.g., W. A. Tidwell, Secret Service, CSA, in D. S. Heidler and J. T. Heidler (eds), *supra*, note 5, Vol. 4, pp. 1722–1733.

[92] See, e.g., W. A. Tidwell *et al., Come Retribution: The Confederate Secret Service and the Assassination of Lincoln* (1988) (University Press of Mississippi, Jackson) at p. 49, and p. 218.

[93] As discussed by R. D. Meade, *op cit*, at pp. 297–305.

[94] See, e.g., R. W. Patrick, *op cit*, at p. 201.

Richmond. Indeed, they were on the same floor "hardly a hundred feet distant".[95] So close was this relationship during this period that one commentator has concluded that Benjamin "was to the civilian government what Robert E Lee was to the military . . .".[96]

During these years "Mr Benjamin lived in a very modest way at the west end of Richmond, with a 'mess', as it was called, of Louisiana Congressmen"[97] including Duncan F. Kenner. According to Littleton Washington, "while he liked intercourse with a few friends, he did not care for crowds or general society"[98]. Though a frequent guest at the Confederate "White House" these tended to be modest and mostly private affairs. With no resident foreign diplomatic corps or visiting foreign ministers, there was little call for official entertaining. Given the Union blockade, there were to be no annual trips to Europe to visit his wife and daughter who remained in France throughout the conflict.

Over time Benjamin became convinced that foreign recognition would never be forthcoming while the institution of slavery remained central to the Confederate project.[99] Similarly, as the war situation progressively worsened the concept of reversing the military tide then flowing strongly in favour of the Union by arming the slaves of the south began to gain some traction.[100] The re-election of Lincoln in November 1864 opened a window of opportunity to progress these radical ideas.

---

[95] *Supra*, note 24, p. 244.

[96] *Supra*, note 52, p. 235. A vast literature exists, and continues to grow, relating to the military exploits and historical importance of General Lee. See generally, e. g., M. Korda, *Clouds of Glory: The Life and Legend of Robert E. Lee* (2015) (Harper Perennial, London).

[97] *Supra*, note 84.

[98] *Id*.

[99] See, e.g., R. W. Patrick, *op cit*, at p. 188.

[100] For a recent work on this topic see, P. D. Dillard, *Jefferson Davis's Final Campaign: Confederate Nationalism and the Fight to Arm Slaves* (2017) (Mercer University Press, Macon, Ga).

Figure 2.3 Benjamin and other "Confederate Chieftains", ca.1864. Buttre, John Chester, Engraver. Confederate chieftains / Engd. by J.C. Buttre, New York, ca. 1864. Photograph. www.loc.gov/item/94509430/.

On the issue of recognition, Benjamin and Davis decided to send Duncan Kenner of Louisiana on a secret mission to France and England to gauge the reaction of these governments[101] to this proposal. Kenner sailed for Europe in early 1865, but even this bold move failed to move the diplomatic needle.[102] As William Davis has recalled, "Napoleon finessed them, as usual, by saying he could not act unless England did so first, and Whitehall simply listened politely to a rather oblique hint of emancipation, and replied that British policy on the American war had not changed, and would not."[103] At much the same time that the Kenner mission was playing out in Europe, Benjamin went public in his support for the proposition that slaves who volunteered to fight for the Confederacy should, in return, be freed. For this, he elected to address a mass white audience at the African Church in Richmond on 9 February 1865.[104]

Reaction to what was to prove to be his last public speech in America was mixed. On 11 February in the Confederate Senate Mr Wigfall introduced a motion of no confidence in Benjamin.[105] Debate was postponed for two days. On the 13th discussion of a revised resolution which recorded that he "is not a wise and prudent Secretary of State, and has not the confidence of the country" resulted in a tied vote and was consequently determined in the negative.[106] About a week later Benjamin offered his resignation to the President who declined to accept it.[107] The

---

[101] Not only did Kenner share the same "mess" in Richmond with Benjamin but they had served together in the Louisiana constitutional conventions of the 1840s and early 1850s.

[102] See, e.g., E. N. Evans, *op cit*, at pp. 274–275, and pp. 278–279.

[103] *Supra*, note 25, p. 376.

[104] See, e.g., R. D. Meade, *op cit*, at pp. 305–308; and E. N. Evans, *op cit*, at pp. 281–289.

[105] See, *supra*, note 68, Vol. IV, at p. 550.

[106] See, *id*, at pp. 552–553.

[107] Discussed, e.g., by E. N. Evans, *op cit*, at pp. 289–290.

issue of slave enlistment continued to be discussed in the Congress. It was, however, too little too late.

As is well known, on Sunday 2 April 1865, General Lee informed Jefferson Davis by telegram that he could hold the line against the enemy no longer and that the government must evacuate Richmond. A brief Cabinet meeting followed, which was attended by Benjamin, at which this advice was acted upon and the decision taken for the Cabinet to remove itself to Danville, some 125 miles to the southwest, by train.[108] This development was not entirely unexpected, and some measures to that end had already been taken. There was a further flurry of activity during which "Secretary of State Benjamin had most of the State Department archives committed to the flames in the street".[109] Amid scenes of some confusion, the train departed that evening; arriving at its destination the following afternoon.

Thereafter the already dismal position of the Confederacy unravelled at some speed. These events have been oft-told and perhaps nowhere more thoroughly than in the 2001 study by William C. Davis entitled *An Honorable Defeat: The Last Days of the Confederate Government*.[110] For present purposes, a bare outline will suffice. Richmond soon fell to the enemy, and on 9 April General Lee surrendered the Army of Northern Virginia to General Grant at Appomattox Court House. Davis and his Cabinet again moved south first to Greensboro, North Carolina, and then to Charlotte. There they learned the news that President Lincoln had been assassinated on 14 April.

While in Charlotte the Confederate President was called upon to consider a draft agreement which had

---

[108] See, e.g., J. E. Walmsley, "The Last Meeting of the Confederate Cabinet" (1919) *Mississippi Valley Historical Review*, Vol. 6, No3, p. 336, at pp. 336–337.

[109] *Supra*, note 25, p. 414. See also, e.g., *supra*, note 39, p. 315.

[110] (2001) (Harcourt Inc, New York).

been reached between Generals Sherman and Johnston – the latter assisted by Secretary of War Breckinridge acting in his capacity as a general officer.[111] Designed to facilitate an overall cessation of hostilities, its terms were far more generous than Davis had expected. He requested that each member of the Cabinet separately commit their advice on it to writing. Benjamin did so on 22 April. To him, the text was "in substance an agreement that if the Confederate States will cease to wage war . . . the United States will receive the several States back into the Union with their State governments unimpaired, with all their constitutional rights recognized, with protection for the persons and property of the people, and with a general amnesty. The question is whether, in view of the military condition of the belligerents, the Confederate States can hope for any better result by continuing the war; whether there is any reason to believe they can establish their independence and final separation from the United States".[112]

Benjamin's analysis of their present circumstances and future prospects was detailed and clear. He concluded: "Seeing no reasonable hope of our ability to conquer our independence, admitting the undeniable fact that we have been vanquished in the war, it is my opinion that these terms should be accepted . . .".[113] While under the Confederate Constitution, he opined, the President did not have the authority to dissolve the nation as proclaimed in Montgomery, as commander-in-chief "[h]e can end hostilities".[114] He should do so and then "resign a trust

---

[111] See, e.g., *supra*, note 25, at pp. 416–417.

[112] *The War of Rebellion: A Compilation of the Official Records of the Union and Confederate Armies* (1895) (Government Printing Office, Washington, DC), Series I, Vol. XLVII, Part III, p. 821.

[113] *Id*, p. 822.

[114] *Id*.

which it is no longer possible to fulfill".[115] Other members of the Cabinet were broadly of like mind.[116]

After a period "Davis finally authorized Johnston to go ahead with beginning the agreements' implementation as soon as Washington gave its approval".[117] It was not to be. The new US President took a harder line than his predecessor might have been minded to do: "Washington rejected Sherman's agreement and ordered him to treat only for the surrender of Johnston's army on the same terms as those given to Lee".[118]

To President Davis, the logical consequence of this development was that the South must fight on. Johnston received orders accordingly. On 26 April he ignored them and surrendered to Sherman.[119] At an earlier stage, Breckinridge had famously remarked: "This has been a magnificent epic. In God's name, let it not terminate in farce."[120] It is difficult, in retrospect, to avoid the conclusion that such a fate was now fast approaching. The Presidential party, on horseback and with a military escort, headed further south shedding several Cabinet members en route.[121] As they continued their journey, members of the escort are said to have speculated as to which of the remaining dignitaries in their charge would evade capture: "almost universal opinion was that [Benjamin] would fall into enemy hands in a chase".[122]

In early May upon crossing the Savannah River into Georgia Benjamin finally took his leave. In a letter written

---

[115] *Id*, p. 823.
[116] See, e.g., W. C. Davis, *supra*, note 110, at pp. 185–190. For an account of the very similar view taken by Attorney General George Davis see, Neff, *supra*, note 75, at pp. 208–209.
[117] *Supra*, note 25, p. 418.
[118] *Supra*, note 110, p. 193.
[119] See, e.g., R. W. Patrick, *op cit*, at p. 352.
[120] *Supra*, note 110, p. 46.
[121] See, e.g., R. W. Patrick, *op cit*, at p. 352.
[122] *Supra*, note 110, p. 205.

some months later, and reproduced in full at Appendix 1 of this study, he emphasised to his friend James A. Bayard, Jr that this had been done with the full consent of the President. The plan at the time had been that he would proceed along "to the Florida Coast, cross to the Islands, give the necessary orders and instructions to all our foreign agents and rejoin him in Texas, <u>via</u> Matamoros".

At much the same time, public sentiment in the North, stimulated by suggestions of Confederate complicity in the assassination of Lincoln, had turned increasingly hostile. By way of illustration, on 1 May the *New York Times* called for rebel leaders, including Benjamin, to be "consigned to infamy" through the imposition of the penalty of death. In its words: "The leading traitors should die the most disgraceful death known to our civilization – death on the gallows. Their careers should always be associated with that infamous end".[123] The following day President Andrew Johnson, by Proclamation, offered a $100,000 reward for the arrest of Jefferson Davis on account of his alleged involvement in the assassination of Lincoln.[124] Several others – but not Benjamin – were made subject to lower bounties for the same reason.[125] Benjamin, due in large measure to his responsibilities for secret service activities, had good reason to fear that he might also be thought to be implicated in some way.[126]

This spirit of Northern vengeance is well captured in Figure 2.4. A cartoon from 1865, it shows Jefferson Davis hanging from a "Sour Apple Tree". To his right is a line of senior Confederate figures awaiting the same fate (in turn Lee, Breckinridge, Benjamin, Yancey, Toombs, and Wigfall. The assassin John Wilkes Booth is shown joining

---

[123] *New York Times*, 1 May 1865, p. 4.
[124] See, 13 Stat. 756 (1865). See also, *New York Times*, 4 May 1865, p. 4.
[125] See, *id.*
[126] See, e.g., J. M. McPherson, Destroyed Utterly, in *Times Literary Supplement* (London), 1 February 2002, p. 7.

Figure 2.4 Benjamin: Northern demands for vengeance illustrated, 1865. Porah, Charles, and Burgoo Zac. Freedom's immortal triumph! Finale of the Jeff Davis Die-nasty." Last scene of all, that ends this strange eventful history. Confederate States of America, 1865. Photograph. www.loc.gov/item/2008661688/.

the queue). In the top right "the recently assassinated Abraham Lincoln is escorted heavenward by angels".[127]

On 10 May Union troops secured the arrest of Davis near Irwinville, Georgia and took him to Fort Monroe, in Hampton Roads, Virginia. There he would eventually be indicted for treason.[128] On the same day, the British

---

[127] From the summary in the Library of Congress catalogue. See Figure 2.4.
[128] For an excellent recent analysis see, C. Nicoletti, *Secession on Trial: The Treason Prosecution of Jefferson Davis* (2017) (Cambridge University Press, New York). Others would follow. For instance, on 7 June 1865 a further 37 prominent Confederates were indicted for treason but Benjamin, still on the run, was not among them. See, J. Reeves, *The Lost Indictment of Robert E. Lee* (2018) (Rowman and Littlefield, Lanham, Maryland) at Ch.3, Table 3.1. Davis and Breckinridge, who had been so indicted in May were not on the list. See, Reeves, Ch.3, text, at note 27. See also, *New York Times*, 27 May 1865, at p. 1.

Ambassador in Washington informed the British Foreign Secretary that: "It is undoubtedly true that the Confederate Government has ceased to exist, that its organized armies have surrendered and that men taken in arms hereafter resisting the authority of the Government will be treated as Brigands."[129]

Benjamin soon learned of the capture of Davis and knew at once that he was now a lone fugitive who would have to fend for himself. As his 20 October letter to Bayard makes clear, he was determined, no matter what the risk, to escape America and find sanctuary abroad. The details of that long and dangerous journey, and its unlikely outcome, are set out in his own words in Appendix 1. The text reads almost like a work of fiction. His flight to safety involved travelling incognito and on horseback to the Florida Gulf coast – itself no easy thing for one so well known and whose image had for years appeared on the now worthless Confederate $2 note[130] (Figures 2.2 and 5.3)– going into hiding, eventually making a long and challenging voyage in a small open boat to the Bahamas, and from there finding passage to England via Cuba and the island of St Thomas. The great escape would take several months to complete.

It is of relevance to note that while throughout this pro-longed period the US authorities remained on the alert for him and others, the British lost interest. While following the capture of Davis, political reporting from the Embassy in Washington to London continued at fever pitch it essentially ignored the fate of Benjamin and other (former) members of the Confederate Cabinet.[131] The sole focus

---

[129] Despatch No. 287, 10 May 1865, in National Archives, London, FO5/1018.

[130] See, e.g., D. S. Heidler and J. T. Heidler, Currency, CSA, in D. S. Heidler and J. T. Heidler (eds), *supra*, note 5, at pp. 529–530. See also Figure 5.3.

[131] On 19 May 1865 the British Ambassador had informed the Foreign Secretary as follows: "But now no Confederate Government exists even

was rather on how best to repair relations with the United States and the associated need to address irritants in that relationship such as withdrawal of recognition of the belligerent status of vessels of the Confederate navy still on the high seas.[132] His eventual emergence in the territory of Empire and then England would therefore have been the cause of some surprise on both sides of the Atlantic.

in name, nor can it be properly revived . . . ; the members of the late Confederate Congress and its Civil Officers are either fugitives, prisoners, or have submitted and taken the oath of allegiance . . .". Despatch No. 303, National Archives, London, FO5 / 1018.

[132] Central to the British approach was Despatch No. 218 of 2 June 1865 from the Foreign Secretary to the Ambassador in Washington. It was written following detailed consideration of the US Presidential Proclamation of May that the war was "virtually at an end" and had taken into account the capture of Jefferson Davis and the "fugitive" status of others. Unusually the text had been seen and approved by the British Cabinet and by Queen Victoria in advance. In it the Ambassador was instructed to inform the American government that it had "determined to consider the war which has lately prevailed between the United States and the so-called Confederate States of North America, to have ceased *de facto*, and on that ground they recognize the re-establishment of peace within the whole territory of which the United States before the commencement of the civil war were in undisturbed possession", National Archives, London, FO5 / 1010.

3

Benjamin's Exile and Professional Rebirth

On 30 August 1865, the merchant ship transporting Benjamin from the Caribbean docked at the English port of Southampton. In the words of Horton "[t]he flight from Richmond to English sanctuary had taken 150 days"[1]. Though a wanted man in the United States, his arrival in the UK rendered him safe from returning to face the processes of the American criminal justice system should any proceedings be instituted against him. Extradition between the two countries at that time was regulated by Article X of the Treaty of Washington of 9 August 1842; the so-called Webster-Ashburton Treaty. This provided for only seven listed extraditable offences.[2] Treason and other offences of a political character were not so listed. Great must have been his relief that his difficult flight had been brought to an unlikely though successful conclusion. He later also admitted to having been "rather pleasantly excited by the feeling of triumph in disappointing the malice of my enemies"[3].

---

[1] H. C. Horton, "Judah P. Benjamin: Lawyer Under Three Flags" (1965) *American Bar Association Journal*, Vol. 51, p. 1149 at p. 1152.

[2] Namely: murder; assault with intent to commit murder; piracy, arson; robbery; forgery; or, the utterance of forged papers. That Benjamin was aware of the treaty limitations on extradition from the UK to the US is evident from his pleadings in the *Creole* case of 1845 discussed in Chapter 1. See, *McCargo v New Orleans Insurance Company* 10 Rob.(LA) 202 (1845), at 282.

[3] See, letter from Benjamin to Bayard, 20 October 1865, reproduced at Appendix I.

He was by no means alone in seeking sanctuary in a third state. Many thousands of Confederates also left the United States, heading in the main for exile in Canada, and Central and South America though "[m]ost would eventually return when their bitterness abated"[4]. That said, only one other member of the Confederate Cabinet managed to evade capture by Federal forces and make it to exile abroad. That was General John C. Breckinridge, a former Vice-President of the United States, whom Jefferson Davis had appointed Secretary of War in February 1865; a post he discharged with considerable distinction. He too, with a small group, had made a perilous sea journey from Florida to the Caribbean and thence to safety in Europe.[5] There, however, the close parallels ceased. As one prominent historian has remarked:

Breckinridge lived as an exile for three years, lobbying through friends for a general amnesty that would allow all who might have indictments against them to come home in safety. On Christmas 1868 the amnesty would come, and he went home to Kentucky. Benjamin, on the other hand, would never go back.[6]

---

[4] W. C. Davis, *Look Away! A History of the Confederate States of America* (2002) (The Free Press of New York), p. 424.

[5] See, e.g., W. C. Davis, *An Honorable Defeat: The Last Days of the Confederate Government* (2001) (Harcourt Inc, New York), at pp. 316–392. Breckinridge was also one of the Presidential candidates defeated by Lincoln in the election of November 1860.

[6] *Supra*, note 4, at p. 424. See also, S. C. Neff, *Justice in Blue and Gray: A Legal History of the Civil War* (2010) (Harvard University Press, Cambridge, Mass), at p. 209. Unlike the partial amnesties of 1863, 1864, 1865 and 1867 that issued on 25 December, 1868 was "unconditionally, and without reservation, to all and to every person who directly or indirectly participated in the late insurrection or rebellion, a full pardon and amnesty for the offence of treason against the United States, or of adhering to their enemies during the late civil war, with restoration of all rights, privileges, and immunities under the Constitution and the laws which have been made in pursuance thereof." While this applied to Benjamin and other Confederate leaders some disabilities continued to subsist. See

Upon his disembarkation at Southampton, Benjamin went directly to the de facto Confederate headquarters in central London located at 17 Savile Row.[7] As his friend, and later one of his executors, the Barrister John G. Witt, subsequently recalled, this was an oft trodden path: "Thither came ordinance officers, merchant refugees, purchasers of ships and stores, managers of the Confederate loan, and in later times, after the fall of Richmond in April 1865, war-worn soldiers and politicians"[8]. There he held immediate discussions with James M. Mason, who had been the commissioner of the Confederacy to the United Kingdom, and Colin J. McRae who had been a key Confederate business agent. Both had, in effect, worked for Benjamin as Secretary of State. Mason had also been a colleague in the US Senate prior to secession where he had represented the State of Virginia[9].

It is clear that, notwithstanding the surrender of the Confederacy and the end of the civil war, this group considered itself competent to arrange for the disposition of the remaining limited assets of the London mission. By way of illustration, on 1 September Benjamin wrote to Mrs Varina Davis, the wife of the then incarcerated former President of the Confederate States. It was prompted by an awareness of her difficult financial circumstances following her husband's capture. It reads, in part, thus:

> Knowing as I did how completely your resources had been exhausted before my departure from Georgia,

in particular section 3 of the XIVth Amendment to the US Constitution which entered into force on 9 July 1868. Similarly the Christmas 1868 pardon would not extend to anyone implicated in the killing of President Lincoln.

[7] See, C. MacMillan, "Judah Benjamin: Marginalized Outsider or Admitted Insider?" (2015) *Journal of Law and Society*, Vol. 42, p. 150, at p. 165.

[8] J. G. Witt, *Life in the Law* (1900) (T Werner Laurie, London), at p. 143. Witt was a Barrister as was the second executor of his will, dated 30 April 1883, namely Lindsey M. Aspland.

[9] James Murray Mason served in the US Senate from 1847 to 1861.

I consulted with Mr Mason and Mr McRae, stating that I considered yours was the first and most sacred claim and that one year's salary of Mr Davis ought to be placed at your disposal by sending to you a letter of credit on a London banker. It is but bare justice to both these gentlemen to say that not only did they heartily concur in the justice and propriety of this, but showed me by their correspondence how deeply the whole subject had engaged their warm and earnest sympathy long before my arrival. The only question was whether we could command the means. As I knew however of the need of immediate action, we provided at once for six month's salary and have now at your disposal twelve thousand five hundred dollars, being the President's salary up to 30th June last, which would be sent by this mail if we were confident it would reach you. It will be placed at once to your credit, and we will send you a banker's credit for the amount as soon as we get your instructions about the proper mode of securing your safe receipt of it. I have every hope that we will be able to send you a second remittance of like amount as soon as we can get together the wreck of such means as can still be commanded here, but my time for examination into the condition of affairs here has been as yet so limited that I cannot speak with entire certainty.[10]

As noted earlier in this work, Benjamin knew Mrs Davis well. It is not surprising, therefore, that this letter also ranged over various more personal matters including the circumstances of his escape to the UK from America. In a brief postscript, he outlined his emerging future plans: "I

---

[10] M. Strode, "Judah P. Benjamin's Loyalty to Jefferson Davis", (1966) *The Georgia Review*, Vol. 20, p. 251, at p. 253. Benjamin was also involved in seeking the return of funds seemingly misappropriated by others. See, e.g., W. C. Davis, "The Conduct of 'Mr Thompson'", (May 1970) *Civil War Times Illustrated*, Vol. IX, No.2, pp. 4–7 and 43–47.

have not yet seen my family, but shall go to Paris in a day or two and return the following week. I will probably be a month or two settling up the public business here, and have a project as yet not matured, to commence the practice of law here in London."[11]

A life in London as a lawyer was not the only, or even the most obvious, option open to him. His wife and daughter had for some years, been based in the French capital. Benjamin was a fluent French speaker and had visited on a near annual basis prior to the civil war. His friend, John Slidell, with whom he had served in the US Senate, remained in Paris, where he had been the commissioner of the Confederacy and was extremely well connected.[12] During an early visit "strong inducements were held out for him to establish himself in France"[13]. These Benjamin was minded to resist.

In London he busied himself in networking in political and social circles and in this he was much assisted by Mason and other Confederate contacts. As MacMillan was to note in her 2015 article, "Benjamin was quick to accept sympathetic hands extended to him. A month after his arrival, Benjamin wrote that various members of parliament had called upon him, Benjamin Disraeli offered assistance, and he would dine with Gladstone."[14]

---

[11] Strode, *id.* p. 255.

[12] See, e.g., E. N. Evans, *Judah P. Benjamin: The Jewish Confederate* (1988) (The Free Press, New York), at p. 327 and p. 369. He was a US Senator from Louisiana between 1853 and 1861.

[13] R. D. Meade, *Judah P. Benjamin: Confederate Statesman* (2001 reprint of 1943 original) (Louisiana State University Press, Baton Rouge), p. 326.

[14] *Supra*, note 7, p. 165. It will be recalled that support for the South in the civil war had been widespread in the UK and particularly in England. As has been noted elsewhere: "Support for the South came not only from the business community, but also most of the aristocracy, some of the professional middle classes, members of Oxford and Cambridge universities, Church of England clergymen, officers in the army and navy, and even some working men ..." J. D. Bennett, *The London Confederates* (2008) (McFarland & Co, London), at p. 3.

This was a supportive context which any political exile would greatly envy.

Benjamin, far from seeking a low public profile, also took an early opportunity to contribute to the political debate on the post-war situation in the United States. This took the form of a lengthy letter to the Editor of *The Times* of London which was published on 11 September 1865. It addressed accusations of the maltreatment of Union prisoners of war by the Confederacy and constituted a robust defence of the actions, and the honour, of Jefferson Davis in this context. That letter was reprinted in *The New York Times* two weeks later along with a rejoinder "full of sharp counter-charges".[15] As Evans was to state in his 1988 biography: "It must have been a rude awakening for Benjamin to realize that his every interaction with American public opinion on the war would stir up controversy; it may have contributed to his subsequent reticence on the subject."[16] Indeed so deep was his circumspection on such matters thereafter that upon his death in 1884 the same *New York Times* could conclude that during his life in England "[i]n American politics he took only general interest"[17].

His plans to recommence professional life as a lawyer in England were slow to crystallise. In a letter of 29 September to one of his sisters in America, he noted that "I am almost fixed in my purpose to practice my profession as barrister in London, but have not yet quite decided, because I still lack information about the rules and regulations for the admission of strangers, and the delay may

---

[15] *Supra*, note 13, p. 341.

[16] *Supra*, note 12, p. 355. Benjamin would on rare occasions in future years be provoked into responding to newspaper coverage of civil war related reports concerning himself to which he had taken exception. For the last such intervention see, "Denial by Mr Benjamin", *New York Times*, 29 January, 1884, at p. 1.

[17] *New York Times*, 8 May 1884, p. 1.

perhaps be so great as to deter me. It will also be necessary for me to become naturalized".[18] By mid-November, he was not much further advanced. In a letter to Mrs Davis he stated: "I had intended entering the English Bar, but if, as seems probable, I cannot do so without a novitiate of two or three years at the Inns of Court, I shall have to try something else".[19]

It should be recalled in this context that during the Civil War, the Union had made extensive recourse to the seizure of Southern property. The Second Confiscation Act of July 1862 had specifically targeted all property belonging to designated categories of individuals of interest including Confederate political and military leaders of whom Benjamin was one; his once substantial assets in America were gone.[20] He had, however, been saved from penury by a mix of foresight and good fortune. In his words:

When I first came over I was almost penniless, but very fortunately a merchant friend, a neutral, in whose possession I had placed some cotton, succeeded in sending out to me a hundred bales, which arriving at the highest Liverpool prices, gave me about $20,000. I am therefore

[18] P. Butler, *Judah P. Benjamin* (1907) (Jacobs & Co, Philadelphia), p. 371.

[19] Reproduced in Strode, *supra*, note 10, at p. 257. On 20 October 1865 he wrote to his friend and former Senate colleague James A. Bayard in Delaware thus: "I am preparing for my new life here and hope to be called to the English bar here this winter. There is however as yet no certainty whether the Benchers of Lincoln's Inn will relax in my favour the general rules for the admission of barristers, though my friends speak hopefully on the point". Reproduced at Appendix I.

[20] See, e.g., C. Curran, "The Three Lives of Judah P. Benjamin" (1967) *History Today*, Vol. 17, p. 583,at p. 590. On the issue of the use of confiscation by the Union during the civil war see, e.g., J. M. McPherson, *Battle Cry of Freedom: The American Civil War* (1990) (Penguin Books, London) at pp. 500–503. On the nature and scope of the Second Confiscation Act of 1862, 12 Stat.589, see, Neff, *supra*, note 6, at pp. 123–127. See also, *Miller v US* 78 US 268 (1871). Benjamin's resulting financial difficulties were shared by President Davis and other Confederate Cabinet members. See, e.g., *supra*, note 5, at pp. 206–207.

above want for some years and in the meantime am making up my mind what to do.[21]

There were several major obstacles confronting Benjamin's ambition to resume his legal career in England. Most, but not all, flowed from the absence of any system of reciprocal recognition of foreign professional qualifications. Although in his fifty-fifth year he would need to requalify. The English profession was then, and is now, divided between two primary branches, namely solicitors and barristers.[22] Benjamin had selected the latter as the most appropriate fit with his US background and its emphasis on the representation of clients in court proceedings and in particular on appellate work. In England, access to the Bar was the preserve of the four ancient Inns of Court.[23]

The connected issues of legal education and admission to the Inns of Court had been under increasing scrutiny for some time prior to his arrival in the UK.[24] When, in late 1865, he took the calculated gamble to commit to this course of action these matters were dealt with in the common "Consolidated Regulations" of the four Inns of

---

[21] Strode, *supra*, note 10, p. 257. See also, *supra*, note 13, at p. 327. In addressing the same point in his 20 October 1865 letter to Senator Bayard, Appendix I, he added: ". . . besides which I have made already about ten thousand dollars by means of information furnished by a kind friend in relation to the affairs of a financial institution, in which I invested my little fortune and which has already increased in market value fifty per cent. So you see I am not quite a beggar." The 100 bales of cotton which reached Liverpool in safety was but a small proportion of that which he had entrusted to others for this purpose. See, e.g., *supra*, note 13, at p. 324. It is assumed that the remainder failed to escape the attentions of Union naval assets.

[22] See, e.g., A. T. H. Smith (ed), *Glanville Williams: Learning the Law* (15th ed., 2013), at. p. 227.

[23] The Inns of Court still play a central role in this regard.

[24] See, e.g., "Report of the Royal Commission on the Arrangements in the Inns of Court and Inns of Chancery for promoting the study of Law and Jurisprudence", 1855.

Court of the Trinity Term of that year.[25] The first hurdle was to be admitted as a student for the purpose of being called. There were two routes to this end. First, and perhaps at the time the norm, was automatic admission to those "who shall have passed a Public Examination at any of the Universities within the British dominions ...".[26] This was, in effect, a graduate entry route. All others seeking admission as students were required to satisfactorily pass special examinations in English, Latin and English history.[27] In this context, however, each Inn of Court was afforded the discretion "to relax or dispense with this regulation, in whole or in part, in any case in which they may think the special circumstances so reported, or otherwise ascertained by the Bench, justify a departure from this regulation".[28]

It was the exercise of this discretion which Benjamin sought from the Council of Lincoln's Inn in early January 1866. In his submission, he made, by any measure, a compelling case. He had, he reminded them, been a member of the Bar of the United States for in excess of thirty years and had practiced extensively before the US Supreme Court. He also summarised his political career in the US Senate and thereafter in the Confederate Cabinet including mention of his brief period of office as its Attorney General. He concluded thus: "I am now a Political Exile, proscribed for my loyalty to my own State, which is now again a member of the Union, and have established my residence in London with a view to recommencing the practice of my profession."[29]

---

[25] I am in the debt of Ms C. Williams, Archivist, Institute of Advanced Legal Studies Library, London, for locating the text and sharing the same.

[26] *Id*, s1.

[27] See, *id*, s2.

[28] *Id*, s2.

[29] R. Roxburgh (ed), *The Records of the Honourable Society of Lincoln's Inn: The Black Books* (1968) (Lincoln's Inn, London), Vol. V., p. 133.

Given the obvious strength of his case, it was no surprise that the Council ordered: "under the special circumstances that the Preliminary Examination be dispensed with in the case of Mr Benjamin".[30] It would have been somewhat extraordinary if the decision had been otherwise. That being the case, it is to be wondered why, in his letter, Benjamin had seen fit to mention that he had been "educated at Yale College in the State of Connecticut".[31] While, as previously discussed, he had been something of an academic child prodigy and had "made an excellent record as a scholar at New Haven"[32] the fact of the matter was that he had been expelled by that institution for an indiscretion. True in this instance, he did not claim to be a Yale graduate; indeed, the regulation invoked was, in effect, one for non-graduates. As such, his decision to pray-in-aid his time there with such studied ambiguity is a source of some wonderment. In being so economical with the truth was he in some way seeking a kind of parity of esteem with the many graduates of Oxford and Cambridge who would constitute such a significant part of the student body he wished to join? The matter was not raised by the Council and his motivation is unlikely ever to be clarified.

The next challenge was how to maintain himself and those who depended upon him during his period of study. As Meade has remarked: "He was supposed to meet the residence requirements of six dinners in hall every three-month term for a period of three years; to pay the prescribed fees, and to enter a barrister's chambers in order to learn the methods of practice."[33] None of these activities attracted remuneration.

---

[30] *Id.*

[31] *Id.*

[32] A. P. Stokes, *Memorials of Eminent Yale Men* (1914) (Yale University Press, New Haven), Vol. II, p. 261.

[33] *Supra*, note 13, p. 330.

As to the period of study, Benjamin had formulated a plan which he shared with E. A. Bradford, his former law partner in New Orleans. As later summarised by Evans this "was to study for a year before asking for special admission to the bar rather than ask immediately for a waiver or wait the customary three years. He would thereby comply partially with the requirement and at the same time brush away the intellectual cobwebs regarding the intricacies of English law, familiarizing himself with the courts and various institutions in the legal system."[34] In the meantime, he would meet his personal expenses from the £5 per week he was paid by the *Daily Telegraph* to write a weekly leading article on international affairs.[35] Perhaps fortunately, given his September experience, these appeared anonymously.

The remaining requirement was for Benjamin to secure an unpaid "pupilage" in the Chambers of a senior barrister. In this, he was also fortunate, and in February 1866 he became a pupil of Charles Pollock, QC. He was the fourth son of Sir Jonathan Pollock (Lord Chief Baron of England for near on twenty-five years).[36] As it happens, the father was, in turn, an acquaintance of James Mason.

In an "unfinished fragment" published in 1898 shortly after his death, Charles Pollock (himself later a Baron of the Exchequer) recalled the sequence of events which would see him welcome Benjamin to his large mercantile law practice.[37] Initially, a friend had brought to his

---

[34] *Supra*, note 12, p. 330.

[35] See, e.g., *supra*, note 13, at p. 328. According to the Bank of England's consumer price inflation calculator, £5 in 1866 represents a value of £584.13 in 2019 terms or roughly £30,400 per annum. When admitted as a student Benjamin would also have anticipated drawing on the funds secured from the sale of his cotton the previous year. See, note 21.

[36] See, A. L. Goodhart, *Five Jewish Lawyers of the Common Law* (1949) (Oxford University Press, London), at p. 69, note 11.

[37] See, "Reminiscences of Judah Philip Benjamin: A Fragment by the Late Baron Pollock" (1898) *Green Bag*, Vol. 10, at pp. 396–400.

attention the fact that Benjamin was intent upon being called to the Bar and would be pleased to come to him as a pupil. Having two such individuals in place at the time "I simply declined without giving the subject much thought".[38] Then, in early February 1866, Mason, joined by Benjamin, were house guests of his father:

> The day after this visit, my father, seeing me in court, sent down a note, saying, 'Have you done wisely in declining to take Benjamin as your pupil?' I gave him my reason; to which he replied, 'Benjamin has no need to learn law, all he needs is to see something of the practice of our courts, and to obtain some introduction to the English Bar'. On this, I thought I had been wrong, and fortunately was in time to revoke my first decision, and within a week Benjamin was in my chambers, greedily devouring every paper that came before him, and writing sound opinions.[39]

With such an appropriate pupillage in place, Benjamin's calculated gamble showed every sign of paying off. Yet, as so often in the past, good fortune was to be followed by bad. Benjamin had elected to place a substantial portion of his assets, primarily the proceeds of his cotton export discussed above, with Overend, Gurney and Company; a large and long-established wholesale discount bank. It collapsed into insolvency and suspended payments on 10 May 1866.[40] A financial panic ensued. In the words of Naresh: "It was Benjamin's misfortune to have arrived

---

[38] *Id.*, p. 397.

[39] *Id.*

[40] See, generally, R. Sowerbutts, M. Schneebalg and F. Hubert, "The Demise of Overend Gurney", *Bank of England – Quarterly Bulletin* (2016, Q2), pp. 94–100. This financial institution had been closely associated with the South during the civil war providing, *inter alia*, financing for the construction of blockade runners. See, eg, J. D. Bennett, *supra*, note 14, at pp. 103–104.

from a shattered economy into one that was in a speculative frenzy".[41]

'Black Friday', as the day of the bank's demise became
known, destroyed at a stroke one of the central pillars
upon which Benjamin's plan for the future had been built.
It is perhaps no coincidence therefore that he brought
forward the timing of his formal request to Lincoln's Inn
for the waiver of the normal length of study requirement.
This was embodied in a memorial dated 22 May 1866 and
was considered by the Council on the same day. The text
followed closely, but in greater detail, that of his letter of
January concerning admission as a student outlined earlier;
that is, a summary of his professional and political life in
America. To this, he added mention of his pupilage in the
Chambers of Charles Pollock. Interestingly, subtracted
was all mention of his studies at Yale.[42] The case thus
made by the former "Head of the Cabinet as Secretary of
State for Foreign Affairs" was clear, concise and eloquent.
On the basis of the facts set out concerning his career he
ventured "to hope that you will not consider the rules
which regulate the Call to the Bar of young Gentlemen just
entering into life, as applicable to my case . . .".[43]

Benjamin was more than aware that it is one thing for a
body to possess a discretion and quite another to convince
it that it was appropriate for it to be exercised. Fortunately,
he had uncovered a supportive precedent from some
twenty years previously. It concerned one Charles Richard
Ogden and this he specifically invoked. Ogden was a colourful (indeed somewhat eccentric) lawyer and politician

---

[41] S. Naresh, "Judah Philip Benjamin at the English Bar" (1995–1996) *Tulane
Law Review*, Vol. 70, p. 2487, at p. 2489, note 5.

[42] A partial version of this is reproduced in the published records. See, *supra*,
note 29, at p. 137. I am in the debt of Ms F. Bellis, Assistant Librarian,
Lincoln's Inn for providing me with a digital copy of the complete record
taken from the original being Volume 31 of the *Black Book*, pp. 113–115.

[43] *Id.*

from the British colony of Lower Canada, now constitut-
ing the southern territories of the Province of Quebec. He
had served as the Attorney General of the colony for many
years. Having been removed from office in circumstances
which he regarded as unjust and an affront to his honour
and dignity, he had come to England to petition the
Crown for recompense. While in this self-imposed exile,
he had been offered appointment as Attorney General of
the Crown Dependency of the Isle of Man. Unfortunately
for Ogden under the statute law of that jurisdiction, he
would be precluded, in his particular circumstances, from
assuming that office unless he had been first called to the
English Bar. In 1844 he, therefore, petitioned the Council
of Lincoln's Inn to exercise its discretion and waive the
normal "observances" regulating the Call to the Bar so
he could take up the Isle of Man position. This course of
action, the petitioner prayed, would be justified, *inter alia*,
"taking into consideration the peculiar circumstances of
his case – his advanced period of life (being now in his
54th year), the high position he has hitherto held in his
native Country in the profession and otherwise . . .". The
Council on 22 April of that year so agreed.[44] Ogden died in
February 1866. Some three months later Benjamin was to
urge the Council to adopt the same course of action as in
that earlier "somewhat analogous" case.[45]

His May 1866 memorial also addressed one remaining
and potentially fatal obstacle to his professional ambitions;
namely that of his national status. As Kingham was later to
recall "[i]t was the practice of the Inns of Court from time
immemorial to elect as members only gentlemen who were
subjects of the realm".[46] This requirement still subsisted

---

[44] *The Black Book*, Vol. 24, pp. 341–344. Digital copies of the Ogden materials
were kindly provided by Ms F. Bellis. See note 42 above.
[45] *Supra*, note 29, p. 137.
[46] Letter of 14 November 1932, G. F. Kingham to the Editor (1932) *The Law
Journal*, Vol. LXXIV, p. 334.

in 1866 though it was to be abolished some two years later.[47] In particular "every member of an Inn of Court was required upon his call to the Bar to take the oaths of allegiance and supremacy".[48] It thus fell to Benjamin to satisfy the Council that he was a British subject.

At first blush, it would seem unlikely that, without more, Benjamin would meet this requirement. Since early childhood, his life had been centred in America. He was, without doubt a citizen of the United States[49] and his tenure as a Senator from Louisiana had served as a public manifestation of that status. It will be recalled that Article I, Section 3 of the US Constitution stipulates that "[n]o person shall be a Senator who shall not have attained to the Age of thirty Years, and been nine Years a Citizen of the United States, and who shall not, when elected, be an Inhabitant of that State for which he shall be chosen". That said, both he and his parents had been born abroad. Perhaps in some earlier nexus to the British Crown and in the intricacies of the law and practice of Empire, a solution could be found. As has been pointed out elsewhere, "connections to a state by birth or ancestry are, in principle, both accepted in international law as sufficient to warrant the conferment of that state's nationality. Respectively, these are referred to by the terms '*jus soli*' (right of soil: acquisition of nationality at birth by place of birth) and '*jus sanguinis*' (right of blood: acquisition of nationality at birth by virtue of ancestry)."[50] At the relevant time, the United Kingdom utilised a combination of both in a somewhat confusing mix of common law and statutory norms.

In the nineteenth century, and indeed up to the entry

---

[47] See, Promissory Oaths Act 1868, c.62, s.9.
[48] *Supra*, note 46.
[49] Post American civil war disabilities notwithstanding.
[50] L. Fransman, *Fransman's British Nationality Law* (3rd edition: 2011) (Bloomsbury Professional, Haywards Heath), p. 107.

into force of the British Nationality Act, 1948,[51] the status of British subject was the sole common nationality of those owing allegiance to the British Crown. Several commentators have asserted that Benjamin had acquired this status by birth in 1811 within His Majesty's dominions;[52] that is, within British territory. In the words of Horton: "There was initial concern that Benjamin might not be allowed to practice in England since he was not a British subject – a concern solved when it was pointed out that he was born in the Virgin Islands during the years they were under the Union Jack".[53]

This *"jus soli"* based argument, though commonly applied to Benjamin, is not without serious difficulty. At the time of his birth, the Caribbean island of St Croix was subject to a brief period of British military occupation during the Napoleonic Wars as were its sister islands of St Thomas and St John. Together they constituted an overseas possession of Denmark to which they would be restored by Article III of the Treaty of Peace between the two nations signed at Kiel on 14 January 1814.[54]

At the relevant time, the acquisition of the status of a British territory could, without doubt, be obtained through military conquest. However, as a matter of colonial constitutional law, such military occupation had to be followed by some further act, normally annexation by the Crown.[55] In the words of Sir Kenneth Roberts-Wray, "upon conquest by British arms, a territory is immediately at the disposal of the Crown and will become part of the

---

[51] On 1 January 1949.

[52] See, e.g., *supra*, note 12, at pp. 4–5, and *supra*, note 8, at pp. 164–165. See also, J. Best, "Judah P. Benjamin: Part II: The Queen's Counsel" (2011), *Supreme Court Historical Quarterly*, Vol. XXXIII, No. 3, p. 7, at p. 9.

[53] *Supra*, note 1, p. 1152, note 9.

[54] The islands in question became subject to the sovereignty of the United States in 1917 by way of cession from Denmark at a cost of US$25 million.

[55] See e.g., J. Mervyn Jones, *British Nationality Law and Practice* (1947) (Clarendon Press, Oxford), p. 40.

British dominions on manifestation of the Sovereign's will, by annexation or otherwise".[56] Even were the historical record to provide a basis upon which to argue that in the case of the Danish Virgin Islands these requirements had been satisfied – which is to be doubted – some uncertainty would remain whether at common law the acquisition of the status of British subject would have been automatic.[57]

Perhaps a more convincing argument could be based on ancestry – the *"jus sanguinis"*. The basis for any such claim would revolve around the national status of his parents – and in particular that of his father – at the time of Judah Benjamin's birth. According to Meade, Philip Benjamin (the father) had been born in the West Indian Island of Nevis on or about the year 1781.[58] Sovereignty over it had, as a matter of English domestic law, been acquired by the Crown by settlement in 1628.[59] On this basis, Benjamin, Sr was automatically a British subject from birth.

The above conclusion paves the way for a further, and final, technical legal question: namely, did the law of England bestow the same status on the children of British subjects who were born in foreign countries? This issue "was never definitively settled at common law".[60] Over time, therefore, the matter attracted efforts at clarification by statute.[61] Of particular relevance for present purposes was the British Nationality Act, 1730. This declared and enacted that children born abroad whose fathers were natural-born British subjects were themselves to be the beneficiaries of that status.[62] Given the above, it is unsurprising

---

[56] K. Roberts-Wray, *Commonwealth and Colonial Law* (1966) (Stevens & Sons, London), p. 107.

[57] See, *supra*, note 55, at p. 41.

[58] See, *supra*, note 13, at pp. 4–5.

[59] See, *supra*, note 56, at p. 856. See also, W. Dale, *The Modern Commonwealth* (1983) (Butterworths, London), p. 314.

[60] *Supra*, note 55, p. 36, note 4.

[61] See, e.g., *id*, at pp. 68–69.

[62] Ch.21. The 1730 statute did not specify whether this status could pass

that in his memorial of 1866 Judah Benjamin embraced the concept of acquisition of status by descent and specifically invoked the Act of 1730. He wrote:

> My parents were both natural born British Subjects of British ancestry, and I am consequently a natural born Subject of Her Majesty, although the place of my birth was the Island of St Croix (a Danish possession in the West Indies) during a temporary sojourn of my parents in that Island (4 Geo 2 Ch: 21 s.1)

> I was taken when an Infant to the United States where my father was naturalized during my minority, and I thus became entitled to all the rights of a Citizen of the United States without abjuring my native allegiance.[63]

In other words, he urged the view that he had acquired by descent, and had not subsequently lost, the status of a British subject. As to the latter it should be noted that being British had a somewhat "indelible" quality and this had been the cause of some friction with the United States to which many Britons had emigrated over the years: a package of reforms to address the resulting problems was not agreed between the two countries until 1870.[64]

Benjamin's line of argument on this point went uncontested by the authorities of Lincoln's Inn. As Butler was later to remark "once a Briton always a Briton was an axiom that swept aside, as if they had never been, the forty-odd years of citizenship, and the services in the Senate of a foreign power".[65] Better still from his perspective, the

---

by descent to more than one generation born abroad. This was only addressed by the British Nationality Act 1772 (Ch.21).

[63] This text is not included in the published version, *supra*, note 29. It is taken from the original.

[64] See, e.g., *supra*, note 50, at pp. 142–143.

[65] *Supra*, note 18, pp. 382–383.

Council accepted his petition as a whole, and in what was a most exceptional, though not entirely unprecedented, act of discretion ordered: "Under the special circumstances set forth in the Memorial, the said Judah Philip Benjamin be allowed to offer himself for Call to the Bar in the present Term, and that the further Keeping of Terms, and all other requirements as Qualifications for Call be, in his case, dispensed with."[66] He was so called on 6 June 1866.[67]

Benjamin's gamble had won out. Through this exercise of discretion, he had obtained professional redemption and, given the fate of his investments, the prospects of financial salvation. This, he would not forget. By way of illustration, at his retirement banquet in the Inner Temple Hall on 30 June 1883 he paid the following tribute:

> Lord Justice Turner, Lord Justice Giffard, Lord Hatherly – then Vice-Chancellor Wood, and the late Chief Baron Kelly. These concurred in insisting that I should be dispensed with the regular three years of 'terms' and that I should at once be called to the Bar. I speak only of those who have passed away, and I cannot express the debt of gratitude I owe to them.[68]

Of those still alive, and thus not mentioned by name, the record points to Lord Cairns as having been a particularly influential supporter of this course of action. He was

---

[66] *Supra*, note 29, at p. 137.

[67] See, e.g., *supra*, note 46. It should not be thought, however, that Benjamin was the only "American" to be called to the English Bar. See, e.g., E. A. Jones, *American Members of the Inns of Court* (1924) (St Catherine Press, London), at pp. 231–232.

[68] *The Remarks of the Attorney General and the Response of Mr Judah P. Benjamin at the Dinner in the Inner Temple Hall, London, June 30, 1883* (undated Private Print), Of these Turner (LJ) and Wood (VC) had been on the Council of Lincoln's Inn in May 1866 which exercised its discretion in Benjamin's favour.

Attorney General in 1866 and would subsequently serve the Crown as Lord Chancellor.[69]

The generous treatment afforded to Benjamin by Lincoln's Inn did not meet with universal approval and there was some speculation that political considerations had played a part; *Reynolds' Newspaper*, for one, opined that "there seems little doubt his admission was smoothed by the strong Confederate sympathies of the English bar".[70] On 9 June 1866, *The Jurist*, a periodical for the English legal profession, reported that "[a] number of members of the English bar regard the circumstances connected with the call of Mr Benjamin with feelings of the strongest disapprobation".[71] It continued:

> After his call Mr Benjamin dined at the students' table, and at the close of the dinner – the new made barristers being called up by name to the bar table in order to take desert in the private room of the Benchers – upon the name of Mr Benjamin being called there was considerable applause, not, however, unmingled with very distinct hisses.[72]

At a more formal level in November of 1866 Gray's Inn sent a formal letter to Lincoln's Inn requesting confirmation of the special treatment afforded to Benjamin and asking for "the Grounds upon which they acted".[73] That a separate Inn of Court should have seen fit to intervene in this manner perhaps underlines the exceptional and sensitive nature of the concession which had been afforded

---

[69] See, e.g., Anon, "Judah P. Benjamin" (1889) *Green Bag*, Vol. 1, No. 9, at p. 365.

[70] 3 June 1866, p. 2.

[71] 9 June 1866, p. 238.

[72] *Id.*

[73] Gray's Inn, PEN/4/11, 15 November 1866, p. 95. I am in the debt of Mr A. Mussell, Archivist, Gray's Inn for kindly providing this and related materials.

Figure 3.1 Ostler's Hut Crest, Lincoln's Inn. Reproduced courtesy of the Librarian, Lincoln's Inn.

to him. At its meeting on 26 November, Lincoln's Inn's Council resolved to reply that it had "acted in the exercise of the discretion which has always been considered to be vested in the Bench of each society in special cases; and that the Bench considered Mr Benjamin's position and professional reputation in the United States a sufficiently special reason for Calling him to the Bar".[74] This reply was considered by the authorities of Gray's Inn on 19 December, but no further action was taken.[75] The route to Benjamin's professional rebirth was now unimpeded.

[74] *Supra*, note 29, p. 140.
[75] Gray's Inn, PEN/4/11. 19 December 1866, p. 122.

4

The Rise and Rise of Benjamin the Barrister

Benjamin's expedited call to the English Bar was a necessary but not a sufficient condition for the restoration of his fortunes; confiscated, as seen earlier, by the victorious Union or lost through speculative investment. Several obstacles, professional and substantive, had to be surmounted. As to the former, while it is true that Benjamin was a hugely experienced and respected lawyer in the United States prior to the Civil War, he had been exposed, in a formal sense, to the peculiarities of the English legal system for less than six months. As one commentator has observed:

> At the comparatively advanced age of fifty-five, he had to adapt himself to an entirely new state of things. He had a great deal to learn, and, what was almost as trying, a great deal to unlearn, for although the law of the United States is founded on the English law, time had caused a considerable divergence between them, and the technicalities of practice vary still more.[1]

At a more practical and even more pressing level, he required an appropriate location from which to practice which, in the English system, is not entirely straightforward.[2] As Baron Pollock was later to remark: "It was

---

[1] Anon, "Judah P. Benjamin" (1889) *Green Bag*, Vol. 1, No. 9, pp. 365–366.

[2] See, A. T. H. Smith (ed.), *Glanville Williams: Learning the Law* (15th ed., 2013) (Sweet & Maxwell, London),at pp. 227–228.

some time before he could obtain suitable chambers, but ultimately he settled down in Lamb Buildings, where he remained during the whole period of his practice at the English Bar."[3] More problematic still was the need to attract paying clients. Unlike the position in the United States, these could not approach him directly but only through the intermediation of firms of Solicitors;[4] a branch of the profession with which he had had little interaction since his arrival in England the previous year. For this, Benjamin had a plan.

As early as February 1866 he wrote to E. A. Bradford, his former law partner in New Orleans, that "when called to the bar I shall take the Northern Circuit which includes Liverpool where I hope to get my first start with the aid of some of our old clients there".[5] This was also a city well known for its Confederate sympathies. Upon being called, he gave effect to this intention though at first work, particularly the holding of briefs in court, was slow in coming.[6]

His first court appearance would take place in late February and early March 1867. Briefed by a Liverpool firm of Solicitors, he appeared as a junior for the defendants in "the first important suit by the United States

---

[3] "Reminiscences of Judah P. Benjamin" (1898) *Green Bag*, Vol. 10, p. 396, at p. 398. This was located in the rear of the Pump Court in the Temple, central London.

[4] This was an absolute in Benjamin's time but has been somewhat eroded in more recent years.

[5] Quoted in E. N. Evans, *Judah P. Benjamin: The Jewish Confederate* (1988) (The Free Press, New York), at p. 327.

[6] See, e.g., D. Lynch, "Judah Benjamin's Career on the Northern Circuit and at the Bar of England and Wales" (2011) *The Supreme Court Historical Society Quarterly*, Vol. XXXIII, No. 4, p. 10. On the strength of the ties between Liverpool and the Confederacy see, e.g., J. D. Bennett, *The London Confederates* (2008) (McFarland & Co, London), at p. 3. In a 25 October 1866 letter to James M. Mason Benjamin remarked : "I am as much interested in my profession as when I first commenced as a boy, and am rapidly recovering all that I had partially forgotten in the turmoil of public affairs." Contained in, "Benjamin, J. P., 1811–1884", Miscellaneous Manuscripts Collection, Library of Congress, Washington, DC.

raising questions arising out of the Southern Rebellion ...",[7] namely the *USA v Wagner*.[8] Later the same year he appeared in a somewhat more high profile case arising out of the same conflict and involving his acquaintance, Colin McRae, the former Confederate agent in the United Kingdom.[9] He remained involved in this matter, in which the American government sought an accounting for certain of the assets of the defeated rebel authority, until disposed of on appeal in 1869.[10]

These early cases brought Benjamin welcome exposure in English legal circles. Similarly, his return to court practice did not go unnoticed on the other side of the Atlantic. As the *American Law Review* was to note at the time: "He seems properly to have joined the Northern Circuit, and the secessionist sympathizers at Liverpool ought to give him good business".[11]

Although Benjamin had thus made a steady if unspectacular start to his new professional life more was needed for someone now nearing his late fifties; an 1867 fee income of less than £500 was no basis for a comfortable retirement.[12] Taking the cue from his early years as a

---

[7] G. W. Wilton, "Judah Philip Benjamin" (1907–1908) *Juridical Review*, Vol. 19, p. 305, at p. 318.

[8] *USA v Wagner* (1867) III Equity Cases 724. Benjamin was also involved in the appeal heard in late May and early June 1867. See, *USA v Wagner* (1866–67) II Chancery Appeals 582.

[9] See, *USA v McRae* (1867) IV Equity Cases 327. See also, J. D. Bennett, *op cit.*, p. 156.

[10] See, *USA v McRae* (1867) III Chancery Appeals 79, and *USA v McRae* (1869) VIII Equity Cases 69. As to this litigation see, e.g., J. G. Witt, *Life in the Law* (1900) (T Werner Laurie, London), at pp. 179–182.

[11] (1866–1867) *American Law Review*, Vol. I, at p. 220. In a rare newspaper interview, given in the spring of 1883, Benjamin remarked: "The cause with which I had been identified in the States was, in a certain circle at least, popular here, and the result for me was very helpful." "Judah P. Benjamin: An Interview with the Confederacy's Ex-Secretary" *Atlanta Constitution*, 26 May, 1883, p. 1.

[12] See, e.g., C. Curran, "The Three Lives of Judah P. Benjamin" (1967) *History Today*, Vol. 17, p. 583, at p. 592.

lawyer in Louisiana, he decided to write another legal text. Though the project took somewhat longer to bring to fruition than he had hoped,[13] it was completed in 1868 and published later the same year.

Entitled *A Treatise on the Law of Sale of Personal Property; with Reference to the American Decisions and to the French Code and Civil Law*,[14] it sought to provide comprehensive coverage of that important branch of private law.[15] This was, however, not another mere annotated collection of the relevant case law so common at that time. Similarly, playing to his own Civil Law training in Louisiana, and his familiarity with American precedents, it contained, most unusually, a significant comparative law dimension. Importantly, as MacMillan recently remarked:

> The treatise succeeded because Benjamin went beyond a compendium of cases and provided a dominant conception of the law of sale, constructed upon principles as elucidated in the cases. It was the construction of law by principle, particularly principles common to the Romans and civilians, which was so attractive to readers.[16]

Upon its publication, this book "commanded immediate attention".[17] *The Solicitors' Journal and Reporter*, in its 14

---

[13] See, e.g., R. D. Meade, *Judah P. Benjamin: Confederate Statesman* (2001 reprint of 1943 original) (Louisiana State University Press, Baton Rouge), at p. 336.

[14] (1868) (Henry Sweet, London).

[15] It is divided into five main parts; viz, formation of the contract; effect; avoidance; performance; and breach. For a discussion of the inspiration for the structure used and its longer-term significance see, J. Oosterhuis, "Treatise on the Sale of Personal Property", 1868, in S. Dauchy *et al.* (eds.), *The Formation and Transmission of Western Legal Culture: 150 Books that Made the Law in the Age of Printing* (2016) (Springer, Cham, Switzerland) p. 382, at pp. 383–384.

[16] C. MacMillan, "Judah Benjamin: Marginalized Outsider or Admitted Insider?" (2015) *Journal of Law and Society*, Vol. 42, p. 150, at p. 168.

[17] *The Times*, 9 May 1884, p. 10.

November 1868 issue, was not out of step in characterising it as "one of the most important contributions to legal literature which has appeared for many years".[18] It was also well received in America.[19] Indeed, as Benjamin was to note in the Preface to the second edition in 1873 "[t] he favourable reception given to the work in the United States has encouraged the insertion of a larger number of American decisions . . .".[20]

The appearance of this "near instant legal classic"[21] also brought about a transformation in his professional circumstances. In the words of Goodhart, "[f]rom then on his career was meteoric".[22] Work quickly became abundant and, as Aitken has pithily noted, the "[r]etainers rolled in".[23] His fee income in 1868, the year of initial publication

---

[18] At p. 28. *The Law Times* of 5 September 1868 at p. 350 described it as "one of the most valuable legal publications of the year".

[19] See, e.g., S. Naresh, "Judah Philip Benjamin at the English Bar" (1995–1996) *Tulane Law Review*, Vol. 70, p. 2487, at pp. 2493–2494.

[20] (2nd ed,1873) (Henry Sweet, London). This was the last version for which Benjamin had full responsibility though he was involved with the third edition in 1883. As his editors noted in the Preface, Benjamin "revised and approved the Editor's labours up to the end of the Chapter on Delivery (p.689), when his health gave way, and he was interdicted by his physicians from any further work, and ordered absolute repose and cessation from all intellectual fatigue". This was also the first occasion on which his name appeared in the title. See, A. B. Pearson and H. F. Boyd (eds.), *Benjamin's Treatise on the Law of Sale of Personal Property with references to the American Decisions and to the French Code and Civil Law* (3rd ed: 1883.) (Henry Sweet, London). Following his death five further editions appeared (1888, 1906, 1920, 1931 and 1950). As has been noted elsewhere: "by then, like many nineteenth-century classics, it was showing its age and had begun to lose touch with modern developments in commercial trade and practice". M. Bridge (ed), *Benjamin's Sale of Goods* (10th ed: 2017) (Sweet and Maxwell, London), p. xiii. As will be seen in Chapter 5, this is an entirely new work though one inspired by Benjamin's original.

[21] R. Bader Ginsburg, "From Benjamin to Brandeis to Breyer: Is there a Jewish Seat?" (2002) *Brandeis Law Journal*, Vol. 41, p. 229, at p. 232.

[22] A. L. Goodhart, *Five Jewish Lawyers of the Common Law* (1949) (Oxford University Press, London), p. 12.

[23] R. Aitken, "The Unusual Judah P. Benjamin" (1996) *Litigation*, Vol. 22, No. 3, p. 49, at p. 52.

was approximately £700. By 1873 and the arrival of the second edition it had reached in the near of £9,000.[24] As Meade put it: "At least he was making an income sufficient to support his family and to put something aside for them 'when I am no longer able to work, in the place of what our Northern friends confiscated for [sic.] me'."[25]

This period also saw Benjamin obtain professional preferment or promotion though this was secured more slowly than he had hoped.[26] In 1870 this took the form of being elevated to the rank of Queen's Counsel for the County Palatine of Lancaster.[27] Becoming a "Palatine Silk" – a status which no longer exists – was of considerable potential assistance to his work on the Northern Circuit. This was to be followed in mid-1872 when, at the instigation of Lord Chancellor Hatherley, a Patent of Precedence – another status which has since fallen into desuetude – was conferred upon him.[28] Though not formally an appointment as a Queen's Counsel (QC) it was, to all intents and purposes, the functional equivalent.[29] This was not the first time that Lord Hatherley had come

---

[24] See, *Atlanta Constitution, supra*, note 11.

[25] *Supra*, note 13, p. 349.

[26] See, e.g., *id*, at p. 349.

[27] See, *supra*, note 22, at p. 12 and p. 69, note 14.

[28] See, J. Sainty (ed), *A List of English Law Officers, King's Counsel and Holders of Patents of Precedence* (1987) (Selden Society, London), at p. 282. Benjamin thus took rank at the Bar immediately after Farrer Herschell, QC. Only two further awards of this kind were made thereafter. There appears to have been no holder of a Patent of Precedence since 1897. See, *id.*, at p. 276. See further, the coverage of this development in *The Times*, 5 August 1872, p. 3. In its view "[t]he promotion of Mr. Benjamin will be received with satisfaction by the whole profession."

[29] As has been noted elsewhere: "Holders of Patents of Precedence have the same privileges as King's Counsel, but are able to hold briefs against the Crown, which a King's Counsel cannot do without a licence to plead" H. Ockerby, *The Book of Dignities, containing lists of the official personages of the British Empire, civil, diplomatic, heraldic, judicial, ecclesiastical, municipal, naval and military* (2nd ed, 1893) (W H. Allen & Co., London) p. 349 [sometimes cited as *Haydn's Book of Dignities*]. See also, e.g., *supra*, note 22, at pp. 12–13. Consequently Benjamin's name does not appear in the

to Benjamin's assistance in England. As was noted earlier, as Vice-Chancellor Page Wood, he had been on the committee of Lincoln's Inn which facilitated his call to the Bar in 1866 and had even attended his call ceremony.[30] Not so much a mentor as a guardian angel, Benjamin publicly acknowledged his debt of gratitude to him at his retirement banquet in June 1883.

Benjamin was delighted by this development and wrote to his family at length on the matter. In his words:

> I received it [the patent of precedence] in person from the Lord Chancellor at his own house, and he gave it to me with some very flattering expressions. I need hardly say that as the law journals and the *Times* have contained some articles on the subject it will be of immense value to me in my profession in various ways, both in increased income and in greater facility of labor; for you must know that a 'leader' who has a patent of precedence has not half as hard work as a 'junior', because it is the business of the junior to do all the work connected with the pleadings and preparation of a cause, and the leader does nothing but argue and try the causes after they have been completely prepared for him.
>
> As the ladies always want to know all details of ceremonies, I will say for the gratification of the feminine mind that my patent of precedence is engrossed on parchment, and to it is annexed the great seal which is an enormous lump of wax as large and thick as a muffin, enclosed in a tin box, and the whole together contained in a red morocco box highly ornamented. As nothing of this kind is ever done under a monarchy without an

---

comprehensive listing of QCs and KCs produced by Sainty, *id*. See also, Wilton, *supra*, note 7, at p. 323, note (b).

[30] See in particular, *supra*, note 16, at p. 166.

Figure 4.1 Benjamin as a senior English Barrister. (1907–08) Juridical Review, Vol. XIX, image facing p. 1. CC BY 4.0.

endless series of charges, etc, it cost me about £80 or $400, to pay for stamps, fees, presents to servitors, etc, etc.[31]

The award of the Patent of Precedence "gave a further boost to a career that was already in high gear".[32] His fee income continued to rise steeply and peaked in 1880 at £15,971.[33] Utilising the Bank of England's

[31] Quoted, *supra*, note 13, at p. 350.
[32] *Supra*, note 19, at p. 2494.
[33] See, *Atlanta Constitution, supra*, note 11.

inflation calculator, this is equivalent in purchasing power to approximately £1,887,296 in 2018 terms. Benjamin's ambition to restore his fortunes in British exile had, beyond doubt, met with success.

In a professional sense, the award of the Patent of Precedence in 1872 "allowed Benjamin to specialize in appellate cases";[34] a theme to which we will shortly return. Importantly this shift in focus in his professional life meant that he became increasingly London based, where the relevant appeal tribunals were located, and he spent less and less of his time on circuit in Lancashire.[35] This in turn facilitated more regular contact with his wife and, by now, adult daughter who had remained throughout in the French capital. As Curran has remarked "every Friday evening, he put aside his briefs and travelled to Paris to stay the week-end" with them.[36]

His family had first call upon both his affections and his finances. In the latter context, the demands grew as the years moved on. For instance, in September 1874 his daughter, Ninette, then in her early thirties, married a French Army Officer; one Henri de Bousignac. Benjamin provided a most generous dowry.[37] As the decade progressed, Benjamin built a large mansion in central Paris as the family home. It was located on the Avenue d'Iena, one of the grand boulevards emanating like spokes from the Place de l'Etoile. In the words of Evans:

> The avenue is wide and tree-lined, in Benjamin's day able to accommodate six carriages across, perhaps more. It rises majestically from the Arc de Triomphe to a crest,

---

[34] *Supra*, note 16, p. 169.

[35] See, e.g., J. Best, "Judah P. Benjamin: Part II: The Queen's Counsel" (2011) *The Supreme Court Historical Society Quarterly*, Vol. XXXIII, No. 3, p. 7, at p. 11.

[36] *Supra*, note 12, p. 592.

[37] See, e.g. *supra*, note 13, at pp. 356–357.

from which one looks down a slight decline to his house and a view of the Eiffel Tower, begun the year after his death and completed four years later.[38]

By way of contrast, "[h]is life in London was the simple existence of a bachelor . . .".[39] He rented rooms throughout.[40] From at least 1873 to his retirement he lived in the elegant St James's area first in Ryder Street and thereafter in nearby Duke Street.[41] Both were within easy striking distance of the House of Lords and the Judicial Committee of the Privy Council where his court appearances were increasingly concentrated. Both addresses were also proximate to the Junior Athenaeum Club on Piccadilly in central London of which Benjamin was an active member.[42] A gentlemen's club with an elite membership drawn from the political and professional classes, the universities and the learned societies, among others, this appears to have been the epicentre of his social existence in London. It was a venue where he could dine, relax and entertain. That he was a club stalwart is perhaps implied by the fact that as late as 1929 his portrait continued to adorn its walls.[43]

While his social and professional life was now fully focused on his new existence in Europe, he did not repudiate his past or ignore those with whom he had previously been associated in the Americas. By way of illustration

[38] *Supra*, note 5, p. 383. Place de l' Etoile was renamed Place Charles de Gaulle in 1970

[39] *The Times*, 9 May 1884, p. 10.

[40] In his Will of 30 April 1883 Benjamin confirmed that he possessed "no real estate in England . . .".

[41] See, *supra*, note 13, at p. 352.

[42] As *The Times* was to note in its obituary, 9 May 1884, at p. 10: "He would dine at the Junior Athenaeum, stroll with a cigar in his mouth into the billiard-room or card-room, to see 'the boys' as he called his juniors, play and sometimes engage in a game himself."

[43] See J. H. Winston, "Judah P. Benjamin: Distinguished at the Bars of Two Nations" (1929) *American Bar Association Journal*, Vol. 15, No. 9, p. 643, at p. 646.

"[o]n his five different trips to Europe [Jefferson] Davis always saw Benjamin in London and was entertained by him, the last time in the fall of 1881".[44] That said he refrained from joining so many of his former Confederate colleagues in writing his memoirs or in otherwise involving himself in any significant fashion in American political affairs. He rarely afforded interviews to the media. Above all, he was seemingly content with the realities of his new life. As Littleton Washington, who had worked for Benjamin at the Confederate Department of State in Richmond, was to remark:

> Probably no man in history has borne exile so gracefully or adapted himself so well to new conditions. Meeting him in 1875 in London, I could hardly detect a change in his person, manners and habitual cheerfulness. He did not live in the past. He was always an optimist and was then perfectly happy in his brilliant professional career and its charming associations. Far different had been the fate of those with whom he had been linked in the effort for Southern Independence.[45]

---

[44] H. Strode, "Judah P. Benjamin's Loyalty to Jefferson Davis" (1966) *Georgia Review*, Vol. 20, No. 3, p. 251, at p. 259. As Mrs Davis was later to recall: "On our return to London we saw Mr. Benjamin quite often, and always with increasing pleasure . . . . He appeared happier than I had hitherto seen him, but though he gave Mr. Davis one long talk about Confederate matters, after that he seemed averse to speaking of them. He was too busy to spend much time anywhere, but was sincerely cordial and always entertaining and cheery. His success at the English bar was exceptional, but did not astonish us. In speaking of his grief over our defeat, he said that his powers of dismissing any painful memory had served him well after the fall of the Confederacy." V. Davis, *Jefferson Davis, Ex-President of the Confederate States of America A: Memoir* (1971 reprint of the 1890 original) (Books for Libraries Press, Freeport, NY), Vol. II, p. 810.

[45] D. L. Gibboney (ed) *Littleton Washington's Journal* (2001), Appendix A (entitled "A Memoir of Judah Benjamin" and written in 1897). Rembert Patrick noted a somewhat similar personality trait. He remarked: "For him life was a transition from one job, or case, to another. He gave his

As mentioned above, with promotion came the ever-increasing ability to specialise. Benjamin's decision to concentrate on appellate work not only afforded him the opportunity to focus his personal life in London but also permitted him to play to his professional strengths and away from his one apparent weakness as an advocate; the jury trial. As Goodhart was to remark: "Benjamin was never an outstanding 'jury' barrister, and, in spite of his quickness of mind, cross-examination did not come easily to him, so that with his increasing success he gave up his practice at *nisi prius*, appearing only in the House of Lords, the Privy Council, and the Court of Appeal."[46]

This professional pivot towards appellate cases also permitted Benjamin to turn an apparent weakness into something of a strength; namely, his original legal training in the civil law influenced legal system of Louisiana which in turn flowed from its continental European rather than English colonial past.[47] This was especially so in the Judicial Committee of the Privy Council which acted as the final court of appeal for the British Empire. To it came numerous cases from Quebec and those other possessions of the Crown whose legal systems had their foundations within the civil law tradition. By way of explanation, as a matter of Colonial Constitutional Law in so-called settled

---

all in thought and service to the accomplishment of the purpose of the moment. When the battle ended, win or lose, he shrugged away the past." R. W. Patrick, *Jefferson Davis and his Cabinet* (1944) (Louisiana State University Press, Baton Rouge), p. 201.

[46] *Supra*, note 22, p. 13. By way of contrast his reputation as an advocate in an appeal court context was legendary. As G. W. Wilton remarked "in his own domain he was unsurpassed. In the Chambers of Justice, where suasion in pure and direct argument is supreme, the name of Benjamin as a pleader will go down in the annals of Law." *Supra*, note 7, at p. 332.

[47] See, e.g., *supra*, note 3, at p. 398. In the words of Goodhart, *supra*, note 22, at p. 7: "The law of Louisiana was an odd amalgam of Roman, Spanish, French, and Anglo-American law, so that Benjamin had to acquire a wide knowledge of various legal systems which later proved invaluable to him . . .".

colonies, British subjects took with them the common law and statutory rules in force at the time in England to the extent that they were relevant to the situation of the new colony. By way of contrast, in territories conquered from or ceded by other European colonial powers the pre-existing law remained "in force unless and until it is altered by or under the authority of the Sovereign.".[48] Benjamin's fluency in French and, to a lesser extent, Spanish was also something of an advantage in litigation flowing from certain of these jurisdictions.

This civil law background also assisted, to some extent, in his work in the House of Lords which received certain categories of appeal from Scotland. It, like Louisiana, enjoys a mixed legal system. Scots Law, it will be recalled, has been much influenced by the Roman-Dutch legal tradition. While the many points of difference between them should not be understated there remain significant commonalities.[49] The latter worked to Benjamin's advantage. As one commentator has remarked: "In those days it was

---

[48] K. Roberts-Wray, *Commonwealth and Colonial Law* (1966) (Stevens & Sons, London), p. 541. See also, *Campbell v Hall* (1774) 1 Cowp.204. As the *Times* was to remark in its obituary, 9 May, 1884, at p. 10: "The Privy Council was, perhaps, his favourite tribunal; his wide acquaintance with foreign systems of law qualified him in an eminent degree to deal with the cases from the colonies and dependencies which came before the Judicial Committee in Downing-street."

[49] As Palmer and Reid have remarked: "Due to their Roman and Canon law foundations the systems have a rationally organised taxonomy. The legal discourse of one system is thus readily intelligible to the other. Each recognises the ordering scheme of Gaius and the grammar of Roman categories, and these produce conceptual markers even in areas where considerable Common Law assimilation has taken place. Furthermore, the mixing process within their respective private laws has certain tendencies and patterns, the Common Law penetrating more easily the most porous points of entry, such as delict, while leaving resistant institutions like property law relatively less affected . . . . No division between law and equity . . . has ever been recognised. Civil procedure is adversarial and bears the imprint of Anglo-American influence. Finally, in each case the commercial law has yielded to the economic forces of the national market." V. Palmer and E. Reid (eds.), *Mixed Jurisdictions Compared:*

the custom to brief English barristers in Scottish appeal cases; Benjamin appeared in the majority of them, being helped by his knowledge of Roman law, which is the foundation of Scots Law."[50]

While these factors contributed to Benjamin's extraordinary success in his last decade of practice as a lawyer, they by no means tell the full story. As Naresh has observed:

> It would be unfair ... to characterize Benjamin as a niche practitioner, because that would suggest that his strength lay only in fields in which he was able to recycle his pre-existing knowledge in such a way as to make it useful to him in his new existence. It would be inaccurate, too, because it would undervalue the very substantial part of his practice that dealt with mainstream English law and made a significant contribution to it.[51]

He was involved with broad swathes of private law. "We find him active in cases concerned with shipping, marine insurance, admiralty matters, credit and financing, company law, bankruptcy, contract, and the sale of goods. Benjamin was, at times, involved in cases associated with landed interests, involving real property interests, and succession."[52] His appearances were numerous. As Justice Ruth Bader Ginsburg of the US Supreme Court has noted, "[h]is voice was heard in appeals to the House of Lords and the Judicial Committee of the Privy Council in no fewer than 136 reported cases between 1872 and 1882".[53] It is not surprising, therefore, that in commenting upon

---

Private Law in Louisiana and Scotland (2009) (Edinburgh University Press, Edinburgh), at pp. x-xi.

[50] *Supra*, note 22, p. 13. See also, e.g., *supra*, note 7, at pp. 325–326.

[51] *Supra*, note 19, p. 2501.

[52] *Supra*, note 16, pp. 169–170.

[53] *Supra*, note 21, p. 232.

his retirement in 1883, *The Times* should remark that he had "for many years been almost the leader of the English Bar in all heavy appeal cases".[54] Particularly in the Privy Council he was, without doubt, *primus inter pares*.

Given the broad range of matters with which he was involved during this period it is perhaps surprising that a near consensus has emerged among biographers and other commentators as to his most significant case;[55] namely, *Regina v Keyn* in 1876 arising out of the *Franconia* incident.[56] More surprisingly still is that "[t]his was one of the few criminal cases in which Benjamin appeared as counsel"[57] and, as with the *Creole* case in the Louisiana Supreme Court in the 1840s, discussed in Chapter 1, involved him in the rare consideration of doctrinal concepts concerning the international law of the sea. Appropriately Benjamin shared this view.[58] The *Keyn* case had several dimensions which combined to suggest its selection: it involved complex issues of domestic and public international law; its facts raised matters of high public policy importance; it engaged the interest of the profession and the public; the court was near evenly split; its outcome was controversial; and, it was, in part, swiftly overturned by statute.[59]

---

[54] *The Times*, 9 February 1883, p. 7.

[55] By way of illustration see, e.g., Meade, *supra*, note 13, p. 358; Aitken, *supra*, note 23, at p. 52; Naresh, *supra*, note 19, at p. 2503; and Anon, *supra*, note 1, at p. 366. As *The Times* was to remark upon his retirement: "Among his many arguments, the one most generally known is that which he delivered before the Court for Crown Cases Reserved on behalf of the captain of the Franconia", 9 February 1883, p. 7.

[56] *Regina v Keyn* (1876) 2 Ex.D.63; 13 Cox.CC.403.

[57] *Supra*, note 22, p. 69, at note 11. See also, e.g., Wilton, *supra*, note 7, at p. 324.

[58] See, *Atlanta Constitution, supra*, note 11. In this interview Benjamin remarked: "It was a case in which the entire English bar took the liveliest interest. I never remember them being similarly exercised."

[59] For an interesting and detailed discussion of its importance see, A. W. B. Simpson, *Leading Cases in the Common Law* (1996) (Oxford University Press, Oxford), Ch 9 (entitled "The Ideal of the Rule of Law: Regina v. Keyn (1876)").

It also had a more personal relevance for Benjamin. As he remarked in a rare media interview in the spring of 1883: "The decision brought me not only an extended reputation, but a vast deal of practice".[60]

The case arose out of the collision, on 17 February 1876, of the British merchant vessel, *Strathclyde,* en route to India, and the German steamship, *Franconia,* under the command of Ferdinand Keyn, voyaging between Hamburg and the Danish West Indian island of St Thomas.[61] It took place in the Straits of Dover within three miles of the coast of Kent. As Marston has noted: "The *Strathclyde* sank and in consequence thirty nine persons on board lost their lives".[62]

Several of the victims were taken to England including the port of Deal in Kent and to London thus giving rise to inquests in both places. The first of these was opened by the Coroner at Deal the following day. The jury found that the sinking was caused by the negligence of Captain Keyn who was consequently considered guilty of manslaughter. The second inquest, arising from the landing of three bodies at London docks, had a broadly similar outcome.[63]

It became evident from an early stage that, partly upon the advice of Benjamin, Keyn would argue that the English criminal courts had no jurisdiction to try a foreign national for an offence committed on a foreign vessel on the open ocean.[64] This jurisdictional point was also extensively considered within the UK executive, and the opinion of the Law Officers of the Crown was sought.[65] On 23 March

---

[60] *Atlanta Constitution, supra,* note 11.

[61] See, e.g., *supra,* note 19, at p. 2504.

[62] G. Marston, *The Marginal Seabed: United Kingdom Legal Practice* (1981) (Clarendon Press, Oxford), p. 114.

[63] See, e.g., G. Marston, "The Centenary of the Franconia Case – The Prosecution of Ferdinand Keyn" (1976) *Law Quarterly Review,* Vol. 92, p. 93, at p. 94.

[64] See, *id,* at pp. 95–96.

[65] See, *id,* at pp. 96–100.

the Attorney General of England and Wales, Sir John Holker, the Solicitor General, Sir Hardinge Giffard, and two Crown Counsel opined as follows:

> We are of opinion that the collision between the Franconia and the Strathclyde having taken place within the Territorial Waters of the United Kingdom and the Jurisdiction of the Admiralty, the Captain of the Franconia is amenable to the Criminal Courts of this Country.[66]

In early April Keyn faced trial before a jury for manslaughter at the Central Criminal Court in London. The prosecution team included, among others, the Attorney General and the Solicitor General. The team representing the accused was also numerous but did not at this stage include Benjamin. While the question of jurisdiction was raised in argument the trial judge, Baron Pollock, set the issue to one side for later consideration by the Court for Crown Cases Reserved. The jury then returned a verdict of guilty to the charge of manslaughter.[67]

In early May the jurisdictional question arose for consideration before six judges of the Court for Crown Cases Reserved. Oral argument lasted for four days, that for Keyn being advanced by Benjamin alone.[68] Soon thereafter it became apparent that the bench was divided on the issues at hand. Consequently, the case was ordered to be re-argued before an augmented court of fourteen judges which included "the six before whom it has initially been argued".[69] It sat for six days in June and again the entire oral argument on behalf of Keyn was carried by Benjamin.[70] The range and complexity of the pleadings

---

[66] Quoted by Marston, *id*, at p. 100.
[67] See, e.g., *supra*, note 19, at p. 2505.
[68] See, e.g., *supra*, note 62, at p. 115.
[69] *Supra*, note 19, p. 2505.
[70] See, e.g., *supra*, note 63, at pp. 104–105.

was extensively covered by the media and, in particular, by *The Times*.[71]

A full exposition of the richness of the arguments advanced by both parties lies beyond the scope of a work such as this. A flavour of it can, however, be gleaned from Marston's scholarly summary of the case presented by Benjamin. It reads in full thus:

> His principal argument claimed that the Admiral, in whose jurisdiction the crime was averred to have been committed, had never had the power to adjudicate upon crimes committed on board foreign ships on the high sea. Neither had the King's Bench ever exercised such a jurisdiction. Even if the three-mile belt were part of the realm of England by virtue of the common law or, alternatively or cumulatively, by virtue of the incorporation into English law of a rule of public international law, there was no jurisdiction in any English court to try crimes committed on board foreign ships in these waters since the Admiral was restrained by ancient statutes from adjudicating upon crimes committed within the realm. On the other hand, it was admitted by the Crown that the local courts administering common law had no power of adjudication over crimes committed below low-water mark on the open coast, ie, outside the counties. Legislation was required to confer such jurisdiction and none had been passed which applied to the facts of the present case. In any event, the authorities supporting the claim of the Crown to the property in the seabed and subsoil of the belt were of no relevance

---

[71] In an oft quoted passage *The Times*, in reacting to the final judgement, remarked: "On all accounts, the case will be remembered as one of the greatest ever argued on a point of law, and the arguments and judgements which it has elicited will, we believe, more than sustain the reputation of the English Bar and Bench". 15 November 1876, p. 9. See also, e. g., Wilton, *supra*, note 7, at p. 324.

to the right of property or jurisdiction in the waters above.[72]

The judges took some time to consider their decision and during this period one of their number, Sir Thomas Archibald, died. As is well known in legal circles, in November of 1876 the court split seven to six in favour of Keyn. His conviction for manslaughter was quashed and he walked free. The outcome was both controversial and problematic. As *The Times* was to remark: "The question which was raised in the case of the Franconia is one of very great and of increasing importance, and it is certainly left by the decision in a very unsatisfactory position".[73] It further concluded, "[t]hat the law, as thus declared, can remain unaltered is scarcely conceivable, and difficult considerations may arise in altering it".[74]

The outcome of the Keyn case caused dismay and difficulty within government, and the decision was eventually taken to reverse the outcome as to jurisdiction by primary legislation. This took the form of the Territorial Waters Jurisdiction Act 1878,[75] section 1 of which explicitly vested jurisdiction in the Admiral over offences committed within territorial waters even if committed "on board or by means of a foreign ship . . .". Most unusually, and rather revealingly, the preamble to the Act was couched in declaratory terms; viz, that "the rightful jurisdiction of Her Majesty . . . extends and has always extended over the open seas adjacent to the coasts of the United Kingdom and of all other parts of Her Majesty's dominions to such a distance as is necessary for the defence and security of such dominions".

While this enactment settled, as a matter of domestic

[72] *Supra*, note 62, p. 129.
[73] *Supra*, note 71.
[74] *Id.*
[75] Ch.73.

law, the issue of curial competence in criminal matters within territorial waters, the *Franconia* decision did not thereby become one of mere historical interest. This flowed from the fact that the proceedings had also touched upon the legal status of the seabed and subsoil. In particular, the judgments in *Keyn* came to be regarded by some as authority for the proposition "that at common law Crown territory in general and the realm of England in particular extend no further than the low-water mark on the open coast".[76] This aspect of the case has since resulted in complex litigation in a variety of contexts across the common law world and at the highest levels. *Keyn* has, for example, arisen for consideration with some frequency in cases (particularly in states with a federal structure) concerning the attribution of rights to the oil and gas resources of the continental shelf;[77] a doctrine of both international and domestic law which did not even emerge until the middle of the twentieth century.[78] Benjamin might well have taken pleasure in the fact that over a hundred years after his retirement perhaps his greatest case was still generating significant fee income for members of the legal profession across the globe.[79]

It is of interest to note that what he viewed as his second most important case in English exile was, like *Keyn*, unrelated to the area of commercial law with which his name is today most commonly associated. He called it the "Irish Fisheries case". This was most probably a reference to *Neill*

---

[76] *Supra*, note 63, p. 93, note 2.

[77] See, e.g., *New South Wales and Others v Commonwealth* (1975) 135 CLR 337 (High Court of Australia); *Reference Re Offshore Mineral Rights* [1967] SCR 792 (Supreme Court of Canada).

[78] See, e.g., R. R. Churchill and A V. Lowe, *The Law of the Sea* (3rd ed: 1999) (Manchester University Press, Manchester), at pp. 141–145.

[79] See, e.g., *Re.Seabed and Subsoil of the Continental Shelf Offshore Newfoundland* (1984) 5 DLR (4th) 385 (Supreme Court of Canada). See also, W. Gilmore, "The Newfoundland Continental Shelf Dispute in the Supreme Court of Canada" (1984) *Marine Policy*, Vol. 8, p. 323.

v Duke of Devonshire.[80] It came to the House of Lords in
1882 on appeal from Ireland. This was a complex and long
lasting dispute concerning valuable salmon fishing rights
in the tidal waters of the River Blackwater[81]. This flows
past Lismore in County Waterford "and thence to the sea
at Youghal"[82]. The tide ebbs and flows for a distance of
between twenty and thirty miles. Benjamin, with others,
represented the interests of the Duke and in detailed argument, some engaging issues predating Magna Carta of
June 1215, managed to convince their Lordships to find
unanimously in his favour. To Benjamin, its significance
flowed from the fact that there are numerous such tidal
rivers in Ireland and accordingly the decision had relevance for many of the most important landowners on
that island. It also had the advantage of increasing his fee
income by "in round figures about £10,000"[83]. Meade, in
his biography of Benjamin, also suggests that this constituted his last appearance before the House of Lords[84]. This
is not so. That distinction appears to fall to *Dixon Ltd. v
White*[85] which was argued in early December 1882 some

---

[80] (1882) 8 App.Cas.135. This is more likely than Benjamin's other major
Irish case dealing with fishing rights; namely, *Bristow v Cormican* (1878)
3 App.Cas.641. This concerned fishing rights on Lough Neagh. In this
earlier case Benjamin was not on the winning side. He also acted in
several appeals from Scotland concerning fishing rights. See, e.g., *Lord
Advocate v Lord Lovat* (1880) 5 App.Cas.273. I am in the debt of my
Edinburgh colleague Professor K. Reid for pointing me towards some of
this source material.

[81] As Lord Chancellor Selborne noted, at p. 138: "[I]n this case there have
been two actions and seven trials; three trials in which the juries did not
agree, two in which the verdict was against, and two . . . in which it was
in favour of the Respondent . . . .[Y]ou will probably be of opinion that
this prolonged litigation ought at last to have an end."

[82] Per Lord Blackburn, in a speech of great legal clarity, at p. 175.

[83] *Atlanta Constitution, surpa*, note 11. According to the Bank of England's
CPI inflation calculator his fee was equivalent to around £1,215,000.00 in
2019 terms.

[84] See, Meade, *op. cit.*, at p. 375.

[85] (1883) 8 App.Cas.833. Benjamin's last appearance before the Judicial
Committee of the Privy Council seems to have been in a succession case

four months after he appeared for the Duke of Devonshire. Perhaps appropriately, this came on appeal from Scotland.

Following the award of his Patent of Precedence in 1872, Benjamin received no further formal professional advancement save for his election in 1875 as a Bencher of Lincoln's Inn; a mark of esteem which gave him great pleasure.[86] It might seem curious, given his otherwise "very remarkable" career in England,[87] that he did not obtain high judicial office. While it has been suggested that this may have been due, in part at least, to political sensitivities the truth was perhaps somewhat more mundane.[88] As Wilton has observed: "He would have been a great acquisition to the House of Lords, or to the Judicial Committee, but for either of these tribunals he had not the statutory qualifications until 1881".[89] These were set by section 6 of the Appellate Jurisdiction Act, 1876[90] and included a precondition for appointment of a period of no less than fifteen years as a practising barrister. True he had been qualified since 1876 to hold lesser judicial positions, but these would have required an even more significant loss of income, and it is known that this was an unattractive outcome for him.[91] Thus "[t]o have been a great advocate must be his enduring memorial".[92]

While true, the above characterisation hardly does justice to the scale of Benjamin's achievements during

---

on appeal from Malta; appropriately another example of a mixed legal system. See, *Strickland v Marchese Felicissimo Apap* (1882) 8 App.Cas.106.

[86] See, e.g., *supra*, note 13, at p. 357.

[87] *The Times*, 9 February 1883, p. 7.

[88] On the other hand Benjamin appears to have subscribed to the view that his advancement at the Bar in the early years had been held back by fears that his elevation would have caused offence in the United States. See, Meade, *op cit*, at p. 366. See also, Goodhart, *op cit*, at p. 12.

[89] *Supra*, note 7, at p. 330. See also, Notes (1883) *American Law Review*, Vol. 17, p. 272, at p. 275.

[90] Ch 59.

[91] See, Meade, *op cit*, at p. 366.

[92] Wilton, *op cit*, p. 330.

his comparatively few years of exile in London. As the Attorney General was to recall at the unprecedented banquet held to mark his retirement on 30 June 1883,[93] following the defeat of the Confederacy "he had to bear the usual lot of vanquished men. Little save honour, reputation and great gifts remained to him".[94] Yet in less than two decades, Benjamin had transformed his personal[95] and professional[96] circumstances beyond recognition. Through a mixture of hard work, natural ability and good fortune, among other factors, he had arisen, almost phoenix-like, from the ashes of the "lost cause"; the failed secession of the Southern States.

[93] See generally, Introduction.

[94] *The Remarks of the Attorney General and the Response of M. Judah P. Benjamin at the Dinner in the Inner Temple Hall, London, June 30, 1883* (undated Private Print).

[95] In a rare newspaper interview in the spring of 1883 Benjamin remarked that upon arrival in London "I resolved to make for myself a fortune such as would enable me to spend the last years of my life in carrying out some aspirations I have entertained in the way of writing a law book . . . I have succeeded beyond my wildest hopes". *Atlanta Constitution, supra*, note 11.

[96] As the London *Law Journal* was to remark upon his retirement: "The success of Mr Benjamin at the English bar is without parallel in professional annals". Reproduced in "Notes", (1883) *American Law Review*, Vol. 17, p. 272, at p. 275.

5

Concluding Reflections

When, in early 1883, Benjamin was forced through ill-health to bring his short but glittering career at the English Bar to a close, the news brought forth glowing tributes from both professional colleagues and the quality British press. As noted in detail in the Introduction, the marking of his retirement culminated in an unprecedented banquet, hosted by the Attorney General, at the Inner Temple Hall in London on 30 June of that year.

It will, no doubt, have been a source of personal satisfaction that his retirement was also noted in the United States. In reflecting at length on Benjamin's "remarkable success at the English bar",[1] the *American Law Review* remarked:

> If he were to return to the United States to-day, he would find that eighteen years of peace have sufficed entirely to obliterate the feelings which in 1866, made him a Southerner rather than an American. The professional success which he has achieved in England has been a source of pride to his professional brethren in the United States, in the North no less than in the South. The sympathy which has attended the announcement of his retirement from the bar has been as genuine and spontaneous to the North as to the South of that imaginary boundary which used to be on every man's tongue when he was prominent in our politics, but which is

[1] "Notes", (1883) *American Law Review*, Vol. 17, p. 272, at p. 273.

now scarcely ever spoken of – Mason and Dixon's Line.[2]

Upon his retirement, Benjamin returned to France to be with his wife and family. His medical problems, however, persisted and he eventually passed away, at his mansion in Paris in close proximity to the Arc de Triomphe, on 6 May 1884.[3] He was 73 years of age. Following a funeral service conducted in the same Catholic church where his daughter had been married, he was laid to rest in the Père Lachaise cemetery in the twentieth arrondissement. Located in the north-eastern corner of Paris, this is the largest and one of the most prestigious burial sites in the city. There lie many of the giants of the arts and sciences, of politics and culture. Numerous are the grand mausoleums, the imposing crypts and the elaborate headstones testifying to the importance of their occupants. By contrast, Benjamin rests in a "tomb that for many years after his death bore inscriptions only for the families of St Martin and de Bousignac".[4] Although in 1938 the Daughters of the Confederacy added to it a stone marker recalling some of his major achievements in public life,[5] his final resting place remains one of very real obscurity and near-total anonymity.[6]

---

[2] *Id*, pp. 272–273. This was in marked contrast to the sharp tone with which the same Journal had reported on his 1866 call to that Bar. See (1866–67) *American Law Review*, Vol. I, at p. 220. It had opined, in part, as follows: "No one ever questioned Mr Benjamin's ability. If his moral qualities had been equal to his intellectual, there was no position in his native country beyond his reach."

[3] See, e.g., R. D. Meade, *Judah P. Benjamin: Confederate Statesman* (2001 reprint of 1943 original) (Louisiana State University Press, Baton Rouge), at p. 379.

[4] *Id*.

[5] See, e.g., E. N. Evans, *Judah P. Benjamin: The Jewish Confederate* (1988) (Free Press, New York), at pp. 402–403.

[6] In a similar fashion there are but few public reminders of Benjamin in the United States and none of the grand statues, such as those for a host of Confederate leaders, which currently attract so much negative attention.

Figure 5.1 Author at Benjamin's grave in Paris, 2018

News of Benjamin's death did not go unnoticed in the United States. It generated not insignificant media interest, including restrained but respectful obituaries in the *New York Times*[7] and the *Washington Post*.[8] Jefferson Davis paid

---

[7] "Death of Judah P. Benjamin: The Career of the Secretary of State of the Southern Confederacy", *New York Times*, 8 May 1884, p. 1.

[8] "Judah P. Benjamin: Reminiscences of an Eventful Life which has Just Closed", *Washington Post*, 11 May 1884, p. 3.

Figure 5.2 Stone marker added to Benjamin's grave in 1938.

him tribute describing him as "[t]he pride of Louisiana, the love of all true Confederates ...".[9] On Saturday 10 May some 200 members of the Louisiana legal profession assembled in the State Supreme Court to pay their respects.[10] Gathered beneath the 1853 portrait of Benjamin by Adolf Rinck (Figure 1.1)[11] – which remains today in the collection of the court though not on public display – they recorded resolutions of the New Orleans Bar memorialising his professional achievements.[12] This was followed by

---

[9] *Washington Post*, 18 May 1884, p. 3.

[10] See, *New York Times*, 11 May 1884, p. 2.

[11] See, (Spring 1985) *The Historic New Orleans Collection Newsletter*, Vol. III, No. 2, p. 4.

[12] The current Louisiana Bar Association traces its roots back to 1847, when a group was formed called the New Orleans Law Association. Benjamin was one of those invited to join. See, W. M. Billings, "A Bar for Louisiana: Origins of the Louisiana State Bar Association" (2000) *Louisiana History: The Journal of the Louisiana Historical Association*, Vol. 41, No. 2, p. 389, at p. 391. I am in the debt of Professor J. E. Duggan and his colleague,

an address from Edward Bermudez, the then Chief Justice of Louisiana, in the course of which he remarked:

> It is undoubtedly becoming that the Bar of which he was, for more than a quarter of a century, a bright orna-ment, should mingle its voice with that of his broth-ers across the broad ocean, to honor in him the first American, who from the memorable discovery of this Continent, left penniless the shores of the New World to seek and find fame and fortune in the over-crowded mother-land.[13]

In his adopted country – the land of his perpetual exile – the praise for Benjamin was even more effusive. The *Daily Telegraph*, for which he had written leading articles in his early years in London, discussed in detail his "singularly diversified, exciting and laborious life".[14] *The Times* of London, in a glowing obituary of near unparalleled length, considered "[o]ne of the most remarkable of modern careers . . .".[15] In an oft-quoted passage, it remarked: "His life was as various as an Eastern tale and he carved out for himself by his own unaided exertions not one but three several histories of great and well-earned distinction".

The first of these saw Benjamin's rise from the humblest of backgrounds and the most modest of means to great success at the State and US Supreme Court Bars and the acquisition of associated wealth and position.[16] He was, in this period, very much the embodiment of the American dream. As Chief Justice Bermudez was to remark in 1884,

---

K.Glorioso, of the Law Library at Tulane Law School for providing this information and that contained in the next footnote.

[13] "In Memoriam" (1884) *Reports in the Supreme Court of Louisiana*, Vol. 36, p v.

[14] *Daily Telegraph*, 8 May 1884, p. 7.

[15] "Mr Benjamin, Q. C.", *The Times*, 9 May 1884, p. 10.

[16] See generally, Chapter 1 above.

his life and success "teach the lessons that the highest professional achievements are never the prize exclusively of wealth, protection or other fortuitous incidents".[17] In those early years, Benjamin evidenced many of the personal qualities upon which he would draw throughout: a keen intellect, a gift for foreign languages, something of an ease at social interaction, oratorical skill, a near-limitless capacity for hard work, and an ability to seize upon opportunities as they presented and to exploit them to the full. He also demonstrated considerable resilience; an extraordinary ability to rebound, as with his expulsion from Yale and the loss of his Bellechasse plantation, from adversity. Perhaps the pinnacle of that first career was marked by the apparent offer, in early 1853, of nomination to the Supreme Court of the United States – an honour he declined. As has been pointed out elsewhere: "Had Benjamin accepted and been confirmed, he would have been the court's first Jewish Justice 63 years in advance of the 1916 appointment of Louis D Brandeis".[18]

As noted in detail in Chapter 1 of this study, Benjamin opted instead to take up his seat in the US Senate and thus to prioritise his second, political, career. This was to prove to be the most controversial and the most problematic phase of his public life. It was to be dominated by his defence of slavery, his eventual support for secession and his high profile and influential roles in the

---

[17] *Supra*, note 13, at p vi.
[18] G. Nelson *et al.*, *Pathways to the US Supreme Court: From Arena to the Monastery*, (2013) (Palgrave Macmillan, New York), at p. 85. As Justice Ginsburg was to note in an address for the Jewish Council for Public Affairs on 18 February 2002: "Had Benjamin accepted the Court post, his service likely would have been shorter than the time I have already served as a Justice. In early 1861, in the wake of Louisiana's secession from the Union, Benjamin resigned the Senate seat for which he had forsaken the Justiceship. He probably would have resigned a seat on the Court had he held one, as did his friend Associate Justice John Archibald Campbell of Alabama."

Figure 5.3 Confederate States of America $2 note containing portrait of Benjamin, 1862.

civilian government of the Confederacy. As the Attorney General to Jefferson Davis, Benjamin became a member of the Cabinet – the first person of Jewish heritage to hold such a post in America. More than forty years would elapse before Oscar Straus became the second as the US Secretary of Commerce and Labor under President Theodore Roosevelt.[19] To this day he remains the only Jew whose image has appeared on American currency; the $2 Confederate note. As Evans has reminded us "As a result of the war, Benjamin became the first Jewish figure to be projected into the national consciousness".[20]

Yet though he served the South with dedication and distinction, Benjamin must be allocated his share of responsibility for that failure of political leadership and then of statecraft which brought the country to war and consequent carnage. As McPherson reminds us:

> More than 620,000 soldiers lost their lives in four years of conflict – 360,000 Yankees and at least 260,000 rebels.

[19] Straus served in this capacity from December 1906 to March 1909.
[20] E. N. Evans, "Benjamin, Judah Philip", in R. K. Newman (ed), *The Yale Biographical Dictionary of American Law* (2009) (Yale University Press, New Haven), p. 37, at p. 38.

The number of southern civilians who died as a direct or indirect result of the war cannot be known; what *can* be said is that the Civil War's cost in American lives was as great as in all the nation's other wars combined through Vietnam.[21]

To the extent that the Civil War was a conflict waged to determine the fate of slavery in America, Benjamin, like many others, placed himself on the wrong side of history. More than half a century after the prohibition of the importation of slaves into the United States and the abolition of the slave trade by the United Kingdom and several decades after the abolition of slavery itself in the British Empire, there was a clear moral choice to be made. Benjamin, himself a former slave owner, made his. It should, however, be noted that while for the rest of his life, he remained faithful to the "lost cause"[22] his views on this pivotal matter evolved over time. This is illustrated by a rare newspaper interview given in May of 1883. To the question "Do you say . . . that you believe that if the war of secession had been a success the best interests of the South would have [been] served?" Benjamin replied, in part, thus:

For me the answer to that question is simply to pass into the domain of speculation. I don't know. Fifteen years ago I was in no such doubt. From what I can learn the condition of the South is unavoidable. *So far as the war contributed to the abolition of slavery, I believe it was for good.* So far as it shed the bad blood which had always existed between the North and South, and brought a final settlement to these quarrels – a business

[21] J. M. McPherson, *Battle Cry of Freedom: The American Civil War* (1988) (Oxford University Press, Oxford), p. 854.
[22] See, e.g., *supra*, note 15.

which could have been concluded in no other way – it was for good; but it is not to be so readily admitted that, had the result been different, the prosperity which the North enjoys would not have been possessed by the South.[23]

With the defeat of the Confederate armies and the disintegration of its government, Benjamin, as detailed elsewhere in this study,[24] escaped from America and sought sanctuary in the United Kingdom. In so doing, he entered into the third, final and in many ways most compelling phase of his life story. The magnitude of the challenge facing him in his desire to rebuild his career in the law in English exile has been described in some detail in Chapter 3. His financial situation was precarious, there was no automatic formal recognition of his American legal qualifications, and the part of the profession he desired to join was renowned for its high level of social, and indeed religious, exclusivity.[25] Not everything, however, was against him. As MacMillan reminds us "he was male and white".[26] He was also politically, and to an extent socially, well connected. Though technically British, he presented as a somewhat exotic foreigner; then as now something of a passport to social mobility within the confusing confines of the English class system.

Though the barriers he faced were considerable, Benjamin was to make light of them in later life. When in the Spring of 1883 he was asked whether he had found securing success at the Bar a hard struggle, he replied:

---

[23] "Judah P. Benjamin: Success at the British Bar – His Views on American Affairs", *Washington Post*, 20 May 1883, p. 3. Emphasis added.

[24] See, e.g., Appendix 1.

[25] See, e.g., C. MacMillan, "Judah Benjamin: Marginalized Outsider or Admitted Insider?" (2015) *Journal of Law and Society*, Vol. 42, p. 150, at p. 165.

[26] *Id*, p. 170.

No. I cannot say that I did. I seemed to drift easily enough into practice. Mine, however, was a different experience than falls to the lot of the young English barrister. I was almost fifty years of age and brought to my efforts here the ripe experience of thirty years of active life. The cause with which I had been identified in the States was, in a certain circle, at least, popular here, and the result for me was very helpful.[27]

While, as seen earlier in this study, Confederate sympathies within the legal profession and in English society more generally, no doubt assisted in securing his expedited call to the Bar and facilitated his gaining an initial foothold in practice, it by no means explains the magnitude of the success he was to later enjoy.[28] For that, we must look to both his personal attributes and professional qualities. As to the former, his resilience in the face of adversity was particularly evident in the early part of his English exile. He was from the outset especially determined to rebuild his financial position which had been so shattered by the defeat of the Southern secession. As he was later to remark: "When the end came in America I found myself penniless and in London. It was then I resolved to make for myself a fortune such as would enable me to spend the last years of my life in carrying out some aspirations I have entertained in the way of writing a law book . . . I have succeeded beyond my wildest hopes".[29]

To the drive and determination to realise this financial

---

[27] "Judah P. Benjamin: An Interview with the Confederacy's Ex Secretary", *Atlanta Constitution*, 26 May 1883, p. 1.

[28] See, e.g., S. Naresh, "Judah Philip Benjamin at the English Bar" (1995–1996) *Tulane Law Review*, Vol. 70, p. 2487, at pp. 2497–2498.

[29] *Supra*, note 27. Upon proof of probate on 28 June 1884 his estate in England (thus excluding his property in France where he was domiciled) was valued at £60,221. Utilising the Bank of England's CPI based inflation calculator, this represents some £7,351,000 in 2018 terms. In his Will dated 30 April 1883 he made bequests to his remaining siblings and

goal, Benjamin married his "almost legendary capacity for hard work"[30] to his formidable skills of advocacy which he had honed in his American practice prior to the Civil War. To these, as was seen in Chapter 4, he added an unusual ability "to turn what could be seen as weaknesses into strengths".[31] This is perhaps most clearly seen in the manner in which his training in the mixed legal system of Louisiana paved the way for him to eventually become the barrister of choice in Scottish appeals to the House of Lords as well as those from Quebec, and other similarly complex legal traditions, to the Judicial Committee of the Privy Council.[32]

Benjamin also drew heavily on this rich jurisprudential background in fashioning his 1868 scholarly work, *A Treatise on the Law of Sale of Personal Property; with References to the American Decisions and to the French Code and Civil Law*.[33] Attorneys in mid-nineteenth century Louisiana were expected to possess an unusually broad grasp of legal source material. This is well illustrated by the rule establishing the curriculum for the Bar examinations put in place in November 1840 by the state Supreme Court[34]. In addition to the Code, statutes and jurisprudence of

---

various other relatives. The remainder he left to his wife (Natalie) and his only child (Ninette).

[30] *Supra*, note 28, p. 2499.

[31] *Supra*, note 25, p. 172.

[32] Discussed in Chapter 4 above.

[33] (1868) (Henry Sweet, London).

[34] "The Court will not be satisfied with the qualifications of a Candidate in point of legal learning unless it shall appear by Examination that he is well read in the following Course of Studies at least--Story on the Constitution, The general laws of the United States, Vattel's law of Nations, the Louisiana Code, The Code of Practice, The Statutes of the State, of a general nature, The Institutes of Justinian, Domat's Civil laws, Pothier's Treatise on Obligations, Blackstone's Commentaries, Kent's Commentaries, Chitty or Bayley on Bills, Starkie or Phillips on evidence, Russel on Crimes, and the Jurisprudence of Louisiana as Settled by the decisions of the Supreme Court." Reproduced online by the Law Library of Louisiana as "A Brief History of the Requirements to Join

Louisiana, the "syllabus of readings"[35] which it established extended to "the general laws of the United States"
and specified texts embracing aspects of the civil law,
public international law, and the common law. It can best
be thought of as an expression of the minimum expecta-
tions of the Bench and Bar[36]; a rule that "stood, albeit with
alterations, until the court eliminated it in 1923." [37]

From this firm jurisprudential base, Benjamin was in a
position to bring to bear on this scholarly enterprise the
knowledge and insights acquired in some thirty years of
active legal practice before he sought sanctuary in England.
As noted earlier, upon its publication, the book became a
near-instant legal classic and brought Benjamin greatly
enhanced visibility within the legal profession and consequently much work in the courts. It also, as MacMillan has
noted, "had its own specific impact on the common law.
Two such instances can be seen in the doctrine of mistake
in contract law and the postal acceptance rules concerned
with contractual formation at a distance".[38]

It should not be thought that this excellent and insight-
ful text was by any means the first to address this branch
of the law. Indeed, Benjamin specifically acknowledges
his debt of gratitude to Blackburn's 1845 treatise on the
same subject.[39] Nor, indeed, was it the first, to incorporate

the Louisiana Bar: 1840". Available at <https://lasc.libguides.com/c.
php?g=457651&p=3181841> (last accessed 16 November 2020).
[35] W. M. Billings, "The Supreme Court and the Education of Louisiana
Lawyers" (1985) *Louisiana Bar Journal*, Vol. 33, No.2, p. 75, at p. 77.
[36] See, e.g., E. Gaspard, "The Rise of the Louisiana Bar: The Early Period,
1813–1839" (1987) *Louisiana History: The Journal of the Louisiana Historical
Association*, Vol. 28, No.2, p. 183, at p. 197.
[37] W. M. Billings, "Mixed Jurisdictions and Convergence: The Louisiana
Example" (2001) *International Journal of Legal Information*, Vol. 29, No2,
p. 272, at p. 291.
[38] *Supra*, note 25, p. 168.
[39] C. Blackburn, *A Treatise on the Effect of the Contract of Sale; on the Legal
Rights of Property and Possession in Goods, Wares and Merchandize* (1845)
(William Benning and Co, London).

significant treatment of the principles and practice of jurisdictions from the civil law tradition as William Story's 1847 study well illustrates.[40] It did much, however, to help consolidate the place of, and deepen the emphasis on, comparative private law in subsequent scholarly writings.[41] Beyond that, and as emphasised in Chapter 4, his analytical approach of "the construction of law by principle"[42] separated Benjamin from many of the other legal scholars of the day. As one commentator remarked upon his retirement in 1883: "His knowledge of case-law was no doubt equalled by some of his contemporaries, though it can have been excelled by few. But in his grasp of the leading principles of jurisprudence he possessed a gift as rare as it is valuable, and there are very few modern English law books worthy to be compared with 'Benjamin on Sales'."[43]

Benjamin's study of the law of sale also enjoyed considerable longevity; its eighth and final edition appearing in 1950 some sixty-six years after his death.[44] In the early

---

[40] See generally, W. W. Story, *A Treatise on the Law of Sales of Personal Property with Illustrations from the Foreign Law* (1847) (Charles C. Little and James Brown, Boston). In this, the first comprehensive treatment of this branch of the law from an Anglo-American perspective, "continued reference is made to the Foreign Law, particularly to that of France, which is the most important expression of the law of Continental Europe, and to the Scottish Law, which is a compound of the Roman and the Common Law". *Id*, p viii. As to the Law of Scotland in the early nineteenth century, discussed in comparison to the common law of England and relying generally on the structure utilised by Pothier, see, M. P. Brown, *Treatise on the Law of Sale* (1821) (W and C. Tait, Edinburgh). I am in the debt of my colleague, Professor G. Gretton of Edinburgh Law School, for pointing me in the direction of these source materials.

[41] For a discussion of the broad range of source material utilised by Benjamin in articulating the civil law position see, J. Oosterhuis, "Treatise on the Law of Sale of Personal Property", 1868, in S. Dauchy *et al.*, *The Formation and Transmission of Western Legal Culture: 150 Books that Made the Law in the Age of Printing* (2016) (Springer, Cham, Switzerland), p. 382, at p. 384.

[42] MacMillan, *op. cit.*, p. 168.

[43] *London Daily News*, 30 June 1883, p. 5.

[44] In the view of Oosterhuis, *op. cit*, p. 384. : "Its influence on the law of sales

---

1970s "a team of editors undertook a total rewriting of the book, and the new work, re-titled *Benjamin's Sale of Goods* – which drew on the original *Benjamin* rather more for inspiration than for substance – was published in 1974".[45] At the time of writing this incarnation of his major contribution to legal literature is in its tenth edition.

The fame of the great advocate, as Goodhart reminds us, is intrinsically "ephemeral in character . . .".[46] It is perhaps for that reason that several of the early commentators on Benjamin's life assumed that history would best remember him for his career in the political arena.[47] As the years have passed, however, his legal legacy has endured; somewhat in contrast to his diminishing profile in American political history. That this should be so, flows from the fact that Benjamin was not solely a consummate Barrister, he was also a fine scholar of the law. It is in that combination of factors that the explanation lies for his continued visibility in legal circles within the Common Law world and beyond[48].

of the common law world was profound and far-reaching, particularly because the Sale of Goods Act, 1893, was greatly based on Benjamin's *Treatise*." In his view this facilitated the continued use of his original text and subsequent editions thereafter. Furthermore, "[w]ith minor variations, the Act was copied all over the common law world, demonstrating the high quality and profound influence of the work on which it was primarily based ie, Benjamin's *Treatise*." *Id.*

[45] M. Bridge (ed), *Benjamin's Sale of Goods* (10th edition 2017) (Sweet & Maxwell, London), p. xiii.

[46] A. L. Goodhart, *Five Jewish Lawyers of the Common Law* (1949) (Oxford University Press, London), p. 3.

[47] M. J. Kohler, "Judah P. Benjamin: Statesman and Jurist", (1904) *Publications of the American Jewish Historical Society*, No. 12, p. 63 wrote: "It is primarily as a statesman that Benjamin will live for posterity, for the lawyer seldom lives in history apart from the jurisprudence he may have aided as an unacknowledged factor in developing, while the fame of the orator is most evanescent and fleeting, and rarely is more than a memory for subsequent generations."

[48] Indeed, had he been able in retirement to satisfy the "aspiration", of which he spoke in his May 1883 newspaper interview, apparently to write another legal treatise his reputation in academic legal circles might

Benjamin's life was unusually rich, diverse and complex. It was one of achievements, failures and new beginnings. It was, in many senses, quite exceptional. It was not, by any means, without controversy. This was particularly so in the political arena where his reputation is and will remain tainted by the dark shadow of his influential support for slavery and the associated attempted secession by the Southern States of America. As the *Daily Telegraph* opined upon his death: "Such a career . . . is not likely to be repeated. The man and his circumstances were both unique."[49] It is fitting that this Confederate Jurist should continue to attract attention and to receive periodic and critical re-assessment.

---

have been yet further enhanced. Though the wording used in the interview is somewhat ambiguous this was unlikely to be a reference to the editing of the third edition of his book on the law of sale. The interview was given in May 1883 and the Preface to the 3rd edition is dated February of the same year.

[49] *Supra*, note 14.

Appendix 1

The Great Escape:
Benjamin's Flight into Exile

NOTE: What follows is the complete text of a letter from Benjamin to his friend James A. Bayard Jr,[1] of 20 October 1865, in which he sets out the details of his escape from America following the collapse of the Confederacy.[2]

17 Savile Row
London
20th October 1865

My dear Bayard,

I was gladdened yesterday by the sight of your well known hand-writing, and received at the same time a letter from your son[3] to which I defer my answer for a day

---

[1] James A. Bayard Jr (1799–1880) had served in the US Senate with Benjamin representing Delaware. At the time of this letter, one of many the two exchanged over the years, he was not in that political office. He subsequently again represented his state in the US Senate between 1867 and 1869.

[2] I am in the debt of Mr E. Richi, Curator of Printed Materials, Delaware Historical Society, Wilmington for locating this material, in the Bayard Papers held by the Society, and providing it to me. The circumstances of his flight from America have stimulated some fictionalised accounts. See, e.g., D. Lankiewicz, *Journey to Asylum* (2015) (Needham, Mass.).

[3] This refers to Thomas F. Bayard (1828–1898) with whom Benjamin was also friendly. He succeeded his father as a US Senator for Delaware and served in that capacity from 1869 to 1885. Subsequently he served as US Secretary of State (1885–1889) and as the American Ambassador to the Court of St James (1893–1897).

or two in hopes of receiving from him the news of the safe delivery of the letter sent to our friend's wife.[4]

I observe from your son's letter that you are but imperfectly acquainted with the circumstances of my escape from the U.S. and give you a brief outline, altho' I have been compelled to repeat the story so often that it has become very tiresome to me.

Early in May, just after crossing the Savannah River I proposed to the President that, as we could not communicate with our agents abroad in any other way, I should leave him to pursue his journey across the Country to the Trans-Mississippi and proceed myself to the Florida Coast, cross to the Islands, give the necessary orders and instructions to all our foreign agents and rejoin him in Texas, <u>via</u> Matamoros.[5] The plan was highly approved and as we travelled on towards Washington, Ga, I dropped behind the party and struck southwards into a cross-road, disappearing completely from the whole party, and with no one in the secret of my purpose except the President and Cabinet. To this prudent precaution I owe my safety.

A week later while pursuing my lonely journey on horseback, I learned the capture of the President and family, and knew at once that our last hope of renewing

---

[4] A reference to Mrs Varina Davis (1826–1906), the impressive and influential second wife of Jefferson Davis the then incarcerated former President of the Confederate States of America. Benjamin came to know her well during the Civil War in Richmond. As noted elsewhere in this study he entertained both of them during visits to London in the years following his release from prison.

[5] Matamoros is a town in Mexico located on the southern bank of the Rio Grande directly opposite Brownsville, Texas. It was much used as a port during the Civil War to avoid the Union blockade. See, e.g., D. Liestman, Matamoros, Mexico, in D. S. Heidler and J. T. Heidler (eds.), *Encyclopedia of the American Civil War* (2000) (ABC-CLIO, Santa Barbara), Vol. 3, pp. 1263–1264. As one commentator has observed : "The once somnolent Mexican port of Matamoros . . . mushroomed into a bustling trading center." S. C. Neff, *Justice in Blue and Gray : A Legal History of the Civil War* (2010) (Harvard University Press, Cambridge, Mass.), p. 186.

the struggle in the Trans-Mississippi was at an end. I felt that I was in great danger of capture as my absence from the President's party would at once become known to the enemy and that telegraphic orders could be sent to their different Head Quarters to ensure an early pursuit. I took my course at once. I went to the house of a farmer well known in the neighbourhood for his devotion to our cause, secured the aid of himself and his good wife in procuring clothes made on the farm, just like those he wore, and travelled through neighbourhood roads, avoiding the highways, [under?] an assumed name, in the guise of a farmer seeking for land on which to locate.

Having been informed that the entire Atlantic Coast was in the hands of the enemy who were vigilantly guarding against attempts to escape, and that nothing remained afloat except their vessels on all the Eastern waters of Florida, I made my way to the Gulf Coast, where after infinite delay and difficulty I succeeded in obtaining a yawl boat that had been sunk in a creek for the last two years to conceal it from the enemy, and in engaging the services of two experienced boatmen, who, tempted by a large reward, were willing to expose their lives to the very great hazard of going to sea in an open boat. By the 23rd June I was able to take my departure from a point on the Gulf Coast just below Tampa Bay, and I coasted all 'round the peninsula to the neighbourhood of Indian Key[6] in about fourteen days, stopping occasionally to go ashore and take fish and turtle eggs which were our main resources, as we could procure on starting no provisions fit for keeping at sea. From the neighbourhood of Indian Key we put boldly off into the broad ocean in our little open boat, in hopes to cross the Gulf Stream in some twenty or twenty-four hours as the weather was fine and the distance across not

---

[6] A small and at the time very sparsely populated island in the upper Florida Keys approximately 20 miles south of Key Largo.

The Confederate Jurist

more than sixty or seventy miles. We were bound for no particular point, my purpose being simply to get across the Gulf Stream on to the Bahama Banks, and there I felt sure that at some of the numerous reefs and Islands which fringe the bank, I should find some of the small craft that are constantly engaged in fishing, sponging and wrecking, any one of which would be glad for a suitable reward to take me to Nassau.[7] Unfortunately after being out about 8 to 10 hours, the wind failed us, then veered ahead creating a heavy sea against which my cockle-shell of a boat could make no head-way by beating. We were without charts, had no instrument, but a compass, and I felt with hourly increasing apprehension that the swift current of the Gulf was sweeping us fatally and irresistibly into the North Atlantic Ocean beyond the Bahama Banks, where I would be compelled as the last chance of safety to turn back to the American Coast. To add to my danger I was in the main channel through which the Yankee steamers were pressing northwards and, again and again, did these steamers pass within full view of us and once even within a quarter of a mile. My dread was that they would take us for a shipwrecked party and turn out of their way to save us. Luckily we were let alone and when at last I was almost on the eve of turning my boat back towards the American Shore, a breeze sprung up which enabled us [barely?] to lay our course, and at about 4 o'clock in the morning we made a light, which turned out to be Gun Key, close to the Bimini Islands, and on the northern edge of the Bank. Four hours more of calm or head wind would have carried us beyond the possibility of reaching the banks.

Once on the Bahama Sea, I attempted to steer for Nassau, but after attempting to make progress against a

[7] Nassau, located on the island of New Providence, was the capital of the then British colony of the Bahamas. It had prospered during the Civil War as a key centre for blockade-running. See, Neff, *op. cit.*, at pp. 186–187.

head wind and heavy sea I soon found that there were uncertain and complicated tides and currents on the sea and that I ran great risk of being lost, in the absence of any instrument to determine my position, so I determined as the weather was very threatening to return at once to the Bimini Islands and get passage on some larger craft.[8] After experiencing the severest squalls I ever witnessed, in one of which <u>two</u> large waterspouts passed in succession within a few hundred yards of my boat, I made the Island and took passage next day in a small sloop of nine tons for Nassau. After being out about twelve hours, this little sloop foundered at sea so suddenly as barely to give me time to jump into a crazy little skiff that was in tow. The negro Captain, and two negro sailors did the same. I seized a compass as I jumped over the sloop's stern, one negro seized an oar, and another a pot of rice that had just been boiled for the men's breakfast. The third negro was nearly drowned by getting entangled in the sloop's sponge hook as he swam for the skiff, and was only saved by his clothes being torn off him, so that he got naked into the skiff. The weather was perfectly calm, and the sinking of the sloop was caused by the twisting open of her planks at the stern. This was attributed to her having been rammed too tight with her cargo of sponge which had been wetted to aid in its compression, and of which the elasticity returned as it dried and this forced open the seams. I directed my little skiff's head again for Bimini from which we were distant about thirty or forty miles, and made the negroes skull by turns with our single oar. This continued from ½ past seven A.M. till about eleven, when we discerned the tops of a vessel's masts towards which we steered, dreading every moment that a breeze would spring up and carry off the vessel which had all sails set, and which could not possibly descry our little

---

[8] A distance of approximately 130 miles from Nassau as the crow flies.

boat. Luckily the calm continued and at 5 P.M. we were hospitably received on board H.B.M. Light-House Yacht Brig the Georgina then on a tour of inspection of the different Bahama Light-Houses. I was taken back to Bimini for the second time, hired another sloop, reached Nassau[9], thence Havana and St Thomas, from which last port I sailed for Southampton on the steamer Seine. After being nine hours at sea a fire broke out on the Seine about ten o'clock at night which compelled us to put the ship about and make for St Thomas again. By almost super human efforts, the flames were kept under till we reached St Thomas, with seven feet water in the fore-hold that had been pumped by the hand and steam pumps into the hold, without however extinguishing the fire. After our arrival in the harbor the fire was gotten under by the aid of the crews of the other vessels in the harbor and after a further delay of three days, we again put to sea with everything "ship-shape" and arrived in Southampton on the 30th August, nearly four months after my separation from the President, during which time I had spent 23 days seated on the thwart[10] of an open boat exposed to a tropical sun in June and July, utterly without shelter or change of clothes. I never however had one minute's indisposition nor despondency, but was rather pleasantly excited by the feeling of triumph in disappointing the malice of my enemies. Of course I was often in imminent danger, but as

[9] From Nassau Benjamin wrote to his sister, Mrs Levy, in the course of which he remarked "I arrived last evening only to learn that if I do not depart this morning for Havana, I may be detained a month before I get another chance to leave this island. I am thoroughly exhausted, and need rest, though in perfect health, but I must not yield to fatigue under the circumstances . . ." Reproduced in part in R. D. Meade, *Judah P. Benjamin: Confederate Statesman* (2001 reprint of the 1943 original) (Louisiana State University Press, Baton Rouge), at p. 324.

[10] A "thwart" is a board or strut placed crosswise in a vessel. In a small boat, as in the present context, it is oft utilised as a seat. The term "thwart board" remains in use today especially in fly-fishing circles. I am in the debt of Dr R. S. Gray of Edinburgh for this nautical explanation.

I had deliberately made up my mind to regard even death as welcome escape from capture, I was far less concerned than I had supposed possible or that you can readily believe.

I hope you are duly grateful for this inordinately long narrative which I could not well make shorter.

I cannot describe to you my dear friend how deeply I am touched by the kind and generous offer of yourself and son, and if I needed aid, there is no one from whom I could consent to receive pecuniary assistance sooner than yourselves. Fortunately this is not the case. I was very poor when I landed here, and had barely enough to support my family for a few months. I have been lucky enough to receive however a hundred bales of cotton that have escaped Yankee vigilance and the price here is so high that it has given me nearly twenty thousand dollars, besides which I have made already about ten thousand dollars by means of information furnished by a kind friend in relation to the affairs of a financial institution, in which I invested my little fortune and which has already increased in market value fifty per cent. So you see I am not quite a beggar.

I am preparing for my new life here and hope to be called to the English bar this winter. There is however as yet no certainty whether the Benchers of Lincoln's Inn will relax in my favour the general rules for the admission of barristers, though my friends speak hopefully on the point. I found my wife and daughter are well, and am as cheerful and happy as it is possible for me to be while my unfortunate friends are in such a cruel confinement and my unhappy country in so deplorable a condition.

How delighted I shall be to press your hand on your promised early visit.

Give my best regards to your son and tell him I will write him next week whether I hear from him in the interval or not. Remember me to all our old friends with affectionate memories, and tell <u>Miss</u> Mabel and <u>Miss</u> Florence that I cannot think of them otherwise than as I knew them, the most charming of <u>young</u> ladies.[11]

Very truly and sincerely yours,

J P Benjamin

PS I will put your son's address on this letter, as less likely to attract attention.[12]

---

[11] Mabel and Florence were the two youngest of James Bayard's seven children.

[12] This basic security precaution was used by Benjamin with some frequency in his early period of exile in London.

Select Bibliography[1]

Books and Monographs

————, *Journal of the Congress of the Confederate States of America, 1861–1865* (1904) (Government Printing Office, Washington, DC).*

————, *The Remarks of the Attorney General and the Response of Mr Judah P Benjamin at the Dinner in the Inner Temple Hall, London, June 30, 1883* (undated Private Print).

————, *The War of Rebellion: A Compilation of the Official Records of the Union and Confederate Armies* (1895) (Government Printing Office, Washington, DC).*

Abraham, H. J., *Justices and Presidents: A Political History of Appointments to the Supreme Court* (3rd ed: 1992) (Oxford University Press, New York).

Benjamin, J. P., *A Treatise on the Law of Sale of Personal Property; with Reference to the American Decisions and to the French Code and Civil Law* (1868) (Henry Sweet, London).

Benjamin, J. P., and Slidell, T., *Digest of the Reported Decisions of the Superior Court of the Late Territory of Orleans, and of the Supreme Court of Louisiana* (1834) (J. F. Carter, New Orleans).

Bennett, J. D., *The London Confederates* (2008) (McFarland & Co, London).

Blackburn, C., *A Treatise on the Effect of the Contract of Sale; on*

---

[1] * denotes a multi-volume work

the *Legal Rights of Property and Possession in Goods, Wares and Merchandize* (1845) (William Benning and Co, London).

Bridge, M. (ed), *Benjamin's Sale of Goods* (10th ed: 2017) (Sweet & Maxwell, London).

Brown, M. P., *Treatise on the Law of Sale* (1821) (W. and C. Tait, Edinburgh).

Butler, P., *Judah P. Benjamin* (1907) (Jacobs & Co, Philadelphia).

Churchill, R. R. and Lowe, A. V., *The Law of the Sea* (3rd ed: 1999) (Manchester University Press, Manchester).

Dale, W., *The Modern Commonwealth* (1983) (Butterworths, London).

Dalin, D. G., *Jewish Justices of the Supreme Court: From Brandeis to Kagan* (2017) (Brandeis University Press, Waltham).

Davis, J., *The Rise and Fall of the Confederate Government* (1990 reprint of the 1881 original) (Da Capo Press, New York).*

Davis, V., *Jefferson Davis, Ex-President of the Confederate States of America: A Memoir* (1971 reprint of the 1890 original) (Books for Libraries Press, Freeport, NY).*

Davis, W. C., *An Honorable Defeat: The Last Days of the Confederate Government* (2001) (Harcourt Inc, New York).

Davis, W. C., *Look Away! A History of the Confederate States of America* (2002) (Free Press, New York).

Deak, F. and Jessup, P. C. (eds), *A Collection of Neutrality Laws, Regulations and Treaties of Various Countries* (1939) (Carnegie Endowment for International Peace, Washington, DC).

Dillard, P. D., *Jefferson Davis's Final Campaign: Confederate Nationalism and the Fight to Arm Slaves* (2017) (Mercer University Press, Macon, Ga).

Evans, E. N., *Judah P. Benjamin: The Jewish Confederate* (1988) (Free Press, New York).

Ferris, M. B., *The Trent Affair: A Diplomatic Crisis* (1977) (University of Tennessee Press, Knoxville).

Foreman, A., *A World on Fire* (2010) (Allen Lane, London).

Fransman, L., *Fransman's British Nationality Law* (3rd ed: 2011) (Bloomsbury Professional, Haywards Heath).

Gibboney, D. L. (ed), *Littleton Washington's Journal: Life in*

Bibliography

Antebellum Washington, Vigilante San Francisco, and Confederate Richmond (2001) (n.p.: XLibris).

Gilmore, W. C., *Newfoundland and Dominion Status* (1988) (Carswell, Toronto).

Goodhart, A. L., *Five Jewish Lawyers of the Common Law* (1949) (Oxford University Press, London).

Heidler D. S. and Heidler J. T. (eds), *Encyclopedia of the American Civil War* (2000) (ABC-CLIO, Santa Barbra, Cal).*

Hornby, E. (ed), *Report of the proceedings of the Mixed Commission on Private Claims, established under the convention between Great Britain and the United States of America, of 8 February, 1853: with the judgments of the commissioners and umpire* (1856) (Harrison and Sons, London).

Jones, E. A., *American Members of the Inns of Court* (1924) (St Catherine Press, London).

Jones, H., *Blue and Gray Diplomacy: A History of Union and Confederate Foreign Relations* (2010) (University of North Carolina Press, Chapel Hill).

Jones, J. Mervyn, *British Nationality Law and Practice* (1947) (Clarendon Press, Oxford).

Korda, M., *Clouds of Glory: The Life and Legend of Robert E Lee* (2015) (Harper Perennial, London).

Korn, B. W., *American Jewry and the Civil War* (2001) (Jewish Publication Society, Philadelphia).

Marston, G., *The Marginal Seabed: United Kingdom Legal Practice* (1981) (Clarendon Press, Oxford).

McPherson, J. M., *Battle Cry of Freedom: The American Civil War*, (1990) (Penguin Books, London).

Meade, R. D., *Judah P. Benjamin: Confederate Statesman* (2001 reprint of 1943 original) (Louisiana State University Press, Baton Rouge).

Moore, J. B., *A Digest of International Law* (1906) (Government Printing Office, Washington, DC).*

Neff, S. C., *Justice in Blue and Gray: A Legal History of the Civil War* (2010) (Harvard University Press, Cambridge, Mass.)

Nelson, G. *et al.*, *Pathways to the US Supreme Court: From Arena to the Monastery* (2013) (Palgrave Macmillan, New York).

Nicoletti, C., *Secession on Trial: The Treason Prosecution of Jefferson Davis* (2017) (Cambridge University Press, New York).

McInnes, M. D., *Slaves Waiting for Sale: Abolitionist Art and the Slave Trade* (2011) (University of Chicago Press, Chicago

Ockerby, H., *The Book of Dignities, containing lists of the official personages of the British Empire, civil, diplomatic, heraldic, judicial, ecclesiastical, municipal, naval and military* (2nd ed: 1893) (W. H. Allen & Co, London).

Palmer, V. V. and Reid, E. (eds), *Mixed Jurisdictions Compared: Private Law in Louisiana and Scotland* (2009) (Edinburgh University Press, Edinburgh).

Palmer, V. V., *Mixed Jurisdictions Worldwide: The Third Legal Family* (2nd ed: 2012) (Cambridge University Press, Cambridge).

Patrick, R. W., *Jefferson Davis and his Cabinet* (1944) (Louisiana State University Press, Baton Rouge).

Patrick, R. W. (ed), *The Opinions of the Confederate Attorneys General 1861–1865* (1950) (Dennis & Co, Buffalo, NY).

Pearson, A. B. and Boyd, H. F. (eds), *Benjamin's Treatise on the Law of Sale of Personal Property with references to the American Decisions and to the French Code and Civil Law* (3rd ed: 1883) (Henry Sweet, London).

Peterson, D. L., *Confederate Cabinet Departments and Secretaries* (2016) (McFarland & Co, Jefferson, NC).

Randall, J. G. and Donald, D., *The Civil War and Reconstruction* (2nd ed: 1969) (D. C. Heath & Co, Lexington, Mass).

Reeves, J., *The Lost Indictment of Robert E. Lee* (2018) (Rowman and Littlefield, Lanham, Maryland).

Roberts-Wray, K., *Commonwealth and Colonial Law* (1966) (Stevens & Sons, London).

Robinson, W. R., Jr., *Justice in Grey: A History of the Judicial System of the Confederate States* (1941) (Harvard University Press, Cambridge, Mass).

Rosen, R. N., *The Jewish Confederates* (2000) (University of South Carolina Press, Columbia SC).

Roxburgh, R. (ed), *The Records of the Honourable Society of Lincoln's Inn: The Black Books* (1968) (Lincoln's Inn, London).*

Sainty, J. (ed), *A List of English Law Officers, King's Counsel and Holders of Patents of Precedence* (1987) (Selden Society, London).

Schouler, J., *History of the United States of America under the Constitution* (1899) (Dodd, Mead & Co, New York).*

Simpson, A. W. B., *Leading Cases in the Common Law* (1996) (Oxford University Press, Oxford).

Smith, A. T. H. (ed), *Glanville Williams: Learning the Law* (15th ed: 2013) (Sweet & Maxwell, London).

Stokes, A. P., *Memorials of Eminent Yale Men* (1914) (Yale University Press, New Haven).*

Stone, K. F., *The Jews of Capitol Hill,* (2011) (Scarecrow Press, Toronto).

Story, W. W., *"A Treatise on the Law of Sales of Personal Property with Illustrations from the Foreign Law"* (1847) (Charles C. Little and James Brown, Boston).

Swisher, C. B., *History of the Supreme Court of the United States: The Taney Period* (1974) (Macmillan Publishing, New York).

Tidwell, W. A., *et al.*, *Come Retribution: The Confederate Secret Service and the Assassination of Lincoln* (1988) (University Press of Mississippi, Jackson).

Warren, C., *The Supreme Court in United States History* (revised ed; 1926) (Little, Brown and Co, Boston).*

Witt, J. G., *Life in the Law* (1900) (T Werner Laurie, London).

Articles, Notes, Chapters

———, "In Memoriam" (1884) *Reports in the Supreme Court of Louisiana*, Vol. 36, p. v.

———, "Judah P. Benjamin" (1889: September), *The Green Bag*, Vol. I, No. 9, p. 365.

————, "Notes", (1883) *American Law Review*, Vol. 17, p. 272.

————, "Reminiscences of Judah Philip Benjamin: A Fragment by the Late Baron Pollock" (1898) *Green Bag*, Vol. 10, at p. 396.

Aitken, R., "The Unusual Judah P Benjamin" (1996) *Litigation*, Vol. 22, No. 3, p. 49.

Bader Ginsburg, R., "From Benjamin to Brandeis to Breyer: Is there a Jewish Seat?" (2002) *Brandeis Law Journal*, Vol. 41, p. 229.

Best, J., "Judah P Benjamin: 'That Little Jew from New Orleans'", (2011) *Supreme Court Historical Society Quarterly*, Vol. XXXIII, No. 2, p. 6.

Best, J., "Judah P. Benjamin: Part II: The Queen's Counsel" (2011), *Supreme Court Historical Quarterly*, Vol. XXXIII, No. 3, p. 7.

Billings, W. M., "A Bar for Louisiana: Origins of the Louisiana State Bar Association" (2000) *Louisiana History: The Journal of the Louisiana Historical Association*, Vol. 41, No. 2, p. 389.

Billings, W. M., "Mixed Jurisdictions and Convergence: The Louisiana Example" (2001) *International Journal of Legal Information*, Vol. 29, No. 2, p. 272.

Billings, W. M., "The Supreme Court and the Education of Louisiana Lawyers" (1985) *Louisiana Bar Journal*, Vol. 33, No. 2, p. 75.

Bonquois, D. J., "The Career of Henry Adams Bullard, Louisiana Jurist, Legislator and Educator" (1940) *Louisiana Historical Quarterly*, Vol. 23, p. 999.

Butler, P., "Judah P Benjamin", in W. D. Lewis (ed) *Great American Lawyers*, (1909) (John C Winston Co, Philadelphia), Vol. VI, p. 257, at p. 260.

Cunningham, G. D., "Judah P. Benjamin and Secession" (2013) *American Jewish History*, Vol. 97, No. 1, p. 1.

Curran, C., "The Three Lives of Judah P. Benjamin" (1967) *History Today*, Vol. 17, p. 583.

Davis, W. C., "The Conduct of 'Mr Thompson'", (May 1970) *Civil War Times Illustrated*, Vol. IX, No. 2, p. 4.

de Ville, W., "The Marriage Contract of Judah P. Benjamin and Natalie St Martin", 1833, (1996) *Louisiana History: The Journal of the Louisiana Historical Association*, Vol. 37, No. 1, p. 81.

Evans, E. N., "Benjamin, Judah Philip", in R. K. Newman (ed), *The Yale Biographical Dictionary of American Law* (2009) (Yale University Press, New Haven), p. 37.

Gaspard, E., "The Rise of the Louisiana Bar: The Early Period, 1813–1839" (1987) *Louisiana History: The Journal of the Louisiana Historical Association*, Vol. 28, No. 2, p. 183.

Gentry, J. F., "A Confederate Success in Europe: The Erlanger Loan" (1970) *Journal of Southern History*, Vol. 36, No. 2, p. 157.

Gilmore, W., "The Newfoundland Continental Shelf Dispute in the Supreme Court of Canada" (1984) *Marine Policy*, Vol. 8, p. 323.

Horton, H. C., "Judah P. Benjamin: Lawyer under Three Flags", (1965) *American Bar Association Journal*, Vol. 51, p. 1149.

Kohler, M. J., "Judah P. Benjamin: Statesman and Jurist" (1904) *Publications of the American Jewish Historical Society*, No. 12, p. 63.

Korn, B. W., "Jews and Negro Slavery in the Old South, 1789–1865", in J. D. Sarna and A Mendelsohn (eds), *Jews and the Civil War: A Reader* (2010) (New York University Press, New York), p. 87.

Launius, R. D., "Judah P Benjamin, 1811–1884", in *Research Guide to American Historical Biography* (1988) (Beacham Publishing, Washington, DC), Vol. 1, p. 129.

Lynch, D., "Judah Benjamin's Career on the Northern Circuit and at the Bar of England and Wales" (2011) *The Supreme Court Historical Society Quarterly*, Vol. XXXIII, No. 4, p. 10.

MacMillan, C., "Judah Benjamin: Marginalized Outsider or Admitted Insider" (2015) *Journal of Law and Society*, Vol. 42, p. 150.

Marston, G., "The Centenary of the Franconia Case – The Prosecution of Ferdinand Keyn" (1976) *Law Quarterly Review*, Vol. 92, p. 93.

Monroe, E. B., "BRADFORD, EDWARD ANTHONY", in K. L. Hall *et al.* (eds) *The Oxford Companion to the Supreme Court of the United States* (2nd ed: 2005) (Oxford University Press, New York), p. 96.

Monroe, E. B., "MICOU, WILLIAM CHATFIELD", in K. L. Hall *et al.* (eds) *The Oxford Companion to the Supreme Court of the United States* (2nd ed: 2005) (Oxford University Press, New York), p. 633.

Naresh, S., "Judah Philip Benjamin at the English Bar" (1995–1996) *Tulane Law Review*, Vol. 70, p. 2487.

Oosterhuis, J., "Treatise on the Law of Sale of Personal Property", 1868, in S. Dauchy *et al.*, *The Formation and Transmission of Western Legal Culture: 150 Books that Made the Law in the Age of Printing* (2016) (Springer, Cham, Switzerland), p. 382

Palmer, V. V., "Mixed Legal Systems", in M. Bussani and U. Mattei (eds),*The Cambridge Companion to Comparative Law* (2012) (Cambridge University Press, Cambridge), p. 368.

Pearce, J. N., "Decatur House Furnishings 1818–1967" in H. D. Bullock *et al.* (eds), *Decatur House* (1968) (National Trust for Historic Preservation, Washington, DC), p. 25.

Rosen, R. N., "Jewish Confederates", in J. D. Sarna and A. Mendelsohn (eds), *Jews and the Civil War: A Reader* (2010) (New York University Press, New York), p. 227.

Sowerbutts, R., Schneebalg, M. and Hubert, F., "The Demise of Overend Gurney", *Bank of England – Quarterly Bulletin* (2016, Q2), p. 94.

Strode, H., "Judah P. Benjamin's Loyalty to Jefferson Davis", (1966) *Georgia Review*, Vol. 20, p. 251.

Walmsley, J. E., "The Last Meeting of the Confederate Cabinet" (1919) *Mississippi Valley Historical Review*, Vol. 6, No. 3, p. 336.

Wilton, G. W., "Judah Philip Benjamin" (1907–1908) *Juridical Review*, Vol. 19, p. 305.

Winston, J. H., "Judah P. Benjamin: Distinguished at Bars of Two Nations" (1929), *American Bar Association Journal*, Vol. 15, p. 567 (part 1) and p. 643 (part 2).

Wiseman, M., "Judah P. Benjamin and Slavery" (2007) *American Jewish Archives Journal*, Vol. LIX, p. 107.

Wortham, T., "BENJAMIN, Judah Philip", *American National Biography* (1999) (Oxford University Press, New York), Vol. 2, p. 568.

Index